Collecting Vintage Children's Greeting Cards

Identification & Values

MW00818076

Happy Birthday To a Darling Little Niece

Merry Christmas TO A LITTLE GIRL

MARGARET O'BRIEN AS *Beth* IN LITTLE WOMEN

Linda McPherson

COLLECTOR BOOKS

A Division of Schroeder Publishing Co., Inc.

Acknowledgments

There are so many people who contribute in so many ways to a book like this.

I would like to thank my dear friends Norma West, Tish Fisackerly, and Lorraine Haywood for being my cheering section and for the wonderful cards they have added to this book. Thanks to a very special cyber friend, Deb Trochler, who just loves to send surprise packages full of card treasures, and to all the great sellers on eBay who find and list so many wonderful cards. And a special thanks to all the talented people at Collector Books for all the hard work they put into publishing *Collecting Vintage Children's Greeting Cards*.

Front cover, clockwise from center:
Beth from Little Women, 1949, 6" x 5". Marked: Hallmark. **$30.00 – 75.00.** (p. 77); **Girl in Bonnet**, 1945, 4½" x 4". Marked: Hallmark. **$5.00 – 10.00.** (p. 198); **Age 10**, boy and girl having sodas. **$3.00 – 8.00**; **Age 9**, children at play. **$3.00 – 8.00**; **Age 8**, boy and girl beside chalkboard. **$4.00 – 8.00.** (p. 156); **Age 7**, boy with sailboat and girl with doll. **$3.00 – 8.00**; **Santa**. Marked: Hallmark. **$4.00 – 8.00**; **Age 6**, Raggedy Ann and Andy. **$5.00 – 10.00**; **Age 5**, lamb in bonnet. Marked: H.A. Co. **$3.00 – 8.00**; **Age 4**, boy and girl on horse. Marked: Quality Cards. **$3.00 – 8.00**; **Age 3**, Little Pig. Marked: Stanley Greetings Inc. **$3.00 – 8.00**; **Age 2**, Children riding train. Marked: Quality Cards. **$3.00 – 8.00**; **Age 1**, baby and cake, 5¾" x 3¾". **$3.00 – 8.00.** (p. 17)

Back cover, clockwise from center:
Girl in Pajamas, 3" x 5". **$5.00 – 10.00.** (p. 137); **Howdy Doody and Clarabell**, 5¾" x 4¾". Marked: Vira Creations. **$10.00 – 25.00.** (p. 46); **Popeye**, 1929, 4½" x 4¼". Marked: Hallmark. **$5.00 – 35.00.** (p. 46); **The Three Little Kittens**, 6" x 5". Marked: American Greetings. **$4.00 – 12.00.** (p. 95); **Hickory Dickory Dock**. Marked: A Gibson Card. **$4.00 – 12.00**; **Jack and Jill**, 1949, 6" x 5". Marked: American Greetings. **$4.00 – 12.00.** (p. 92); **Little Red Riding Hood**, 1949, 6" x 5". Marked: American Greetings. **$4.00 – 12.00.** (p. 92); **Cinderella**, 1950, 6" x 5". Marked: American Greetings. **$4.00 – 12.00.** (p. 98); **Goldilocks**, 6" x 5". Marked: Fairfield. **$8.00 – 20.00.** (p. 82)

Cover design by Beth Summers
Book design and layout by Mary Ann Hudson

COLLECTOR BOOKS
P.O. Box 3009
Paducah, Kentucky 42002-3009

www.collectorbooks.com

Copyright © 2006 Linda McPherson

All rights reserved. No part of this book may be reproduced, stored in any retrieval system, or transmitted in any form, or by any means including but not limited to electronic, mechanical, photocopy, recording, or otherwise, without the written consent of the author and publisher.

The current values in this book should be used only as a guide. They are not intended to set prices, which vary from one section of the country to another. Auction prices as well as dealer prices vary greatly and are affected by condition as well as demand. Neither the author nor the publisher assumes responsibility for any losses that might be incurred as a result of consulting this guide.

Searching for a Publisher?

We are always looking for people knowledgeable within their fields. If you feel that there is a real need for a book on your collectible subject and have a large comprehensive collection, contact Collector Books.

Contents

Introduction

The greeting card as we know it today evolved over centuries. Christmas cards and Valentines were used in the eighteenth and nineteenth century in Europe and were also exported to America. But it wasn't until 1866 when Louis Prang, a Boston printmaker, perfected his Chromolithography process and was able to produce printed images with great detail and in many vivid colors. Beginning with calendars, trade cards, and other advertising, his process of printing was a great success, and in 1874 he began producing Christmas cards. Having the cards printed in America gave buyers much more reasonably priced cards, and soon the tradition of sending Christmas cards to friends and family was available to everyone. Soon other greetings, such as birthday, New Year's, and Easter, were added to the line. Other publishers began using Prang's process, and the greeting card industry became big business.

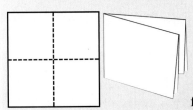

The early cards were still printed in the one-sided postcard format and were often embellished with embossing, glitter, or even fringe. By the early twentieth century, many American publishers were printing greeting cards on sheets of paper that were folded in fourths. The artwork was on the front, and the greeting was inside. The company name, trademark, or code was printed on the back. All this was done by printing on just one side of the paper, a fairly inexpensive way to print. The method of folding in fourths is sometimes referred to as the French fold.

As demand for greeting cards grew, cards for many other holidays and occasions were added to the lines of cards available. Cards that welcomed the arrival of a new baby, or cards for children's first or second (or any other) birthdays were now in demand. The general get well card now had even more specific wishes; cards might wish a child a quick recovery from the pain of having his tonsils removed or from a case of measles or chicken pox.

Cards from the 1930s tend to have fewer, softer, and more muted colors. By the 1940s and 1950s, the trend was for vivid colorful graphics using bright primary colors. Cards from this era were often saved in scrapbooks for children to enjoy for many years. The custom of sending cards was not just for adults; many cards were available for children to send to family and friends. Cards to wish a happy Mother's Day or happy cousin's birthday, or a valentine for Grandma — the choices continued to grow.

The 1960s brought us hippies, psychedelic colors, modern art styles, and other changes in the world, all reflected by the cards from this era. Cards that resembled the styles of those from the 1940s and 1950s were considered nostalgia cards.

This book will give you many examples of those nostalgic cards from the 1930s to the 1960s, with even a few from more modern times. Cards that were sent to children, had subjects that appealed to children, or were sent by children are included.

The topics included here reflect but a small number of those in the marketplace. My goal is to give the reader an idea of ways one might choose to file one's cards. You almost have to limit your collection to one or a few topics, or you will have thousands of cards very quickly. You might want to limit your collection to just baby cards or numbered birthday cards, or those that picture dogs, cats, or other animals. You may like the work of a favorite artist, or perhaps cards made by one company, such as Hallmark. The possibilities are endless. Your collection can be as simple or as complex as you choose. The main idea is to just have fun. If it makes you smile, buy it!

Getting Started

Finding vintage cards was once pretty difficult. A few could be found at antique shops, flea markets, or garage sales, but an estate sale was usually the most likely place to find cards. At one time everyone seemed to always have a box or two on hand to send, and most people saved at least a few that were just too pretty or had too much sentimental value to throw away. Those are still good sources for cards, but today, with the Internet and online auctions such as eBay, it's pretty easy to build a fabulous collection. Just about any type of card can be found online.

Prices in this book are what one would expect to pay for a single mint-condition card online. Cards sold in lots of 10, 20, or even 100 would sell for much less per card. Buying in lots is a quick way to increase the size of your collection, but you will also end up with many duplicates or cards that do not fit into your topics.

When shopping online you will find a wide range of prices for the same cards. One day a special card may sell for over $100, and you may see the same card the next week without a single bid. So if you are patient, most cards can be found fairly reasonably. (Of course, there are always exceptions, and if it is truly a rare card expect to pay the price.)

A word to those who are not familiar with eBay. First, it is the most fantastic way of finding anything ever invented; you could shop 24 hours a day and never see it all. It is a reasonably safe way to shop. Feedback is listed on each seller and buyer, and this can tell you how honest a dealer or customer has been in the past. A pretty good indicator of a safe person is a long list of satisfied buyers. You will of course want to contact the seller right away when you win the bid on an item, and pay promptly. This will give you a start on a list of positive feedback of your own.

You may want to watch out for shipping costs. Many sellers don't list what they charge for shipping, and if you don't ask ahead of time you may find that the wonderful card you got for just $1.00 will cost an additional $4.95 or more. Those extra charges would go a long way toward more cards for you to enjoy. Many buyers won't bid if a seller charges more than the actual cost of shipping. Always play it safe and ask before you bid.

Condition of cards is another factor to consider. Many cards were saved in scrapbooks and were glued or taped to the pages. The old scrapbook pages tend to crumble and come apart from the cover. The cards, however, usually remain in excellent condition. So most are removed from the old pages by either the seller or new owner. If the cards were Scotch taped to the pages, the old yellowed tape may come off but leave a brown stain that is next to impossible to remove. Cards that were glued in can usually be removed with little or no damage, with a lot of practice and patience. Many do not object to some scrap or glue residue remaining on the back of a card, since cards are generally put on new, acid-free pages and their backs are not seen.

A note to dealers: Please leave removing cards to the buyer, who may have more time and experience.

Do you prefer cards in mint unused condition or signed by the sender?

This seems to be a matter of personal preference. For many collectors, an added signature (and perhaps note) tell a special story. Someone shopped for, picked out, and sent this card to someone he or she cared about. If you get a scrapbook or find a box of cards that belonged to one family and begin reading the messages written on these cards, you'll feel like you almost know the family. Cards from Aunt Sue and Uncle Joe are suddenly signed "Aunt Sue, Uncle Joe, and little Billy." Through the years other names are added, or cards from Grandma and Grandpa become just from Grandma, and you wonder...It is much better than any TV drama; these were real people. And they loved each other enough to send cards, and those cards were saved as happy reminders of their lives. Collectors often feel privileged to share those memories and can save them for generations to come.

Dating your cards is often mostly guesswork. You soon learn to recognize the many clues that put a card in a certain era. Some of these clues are artist style, type of printing used, and colors used. Items pictured that were popular during a certain time, or the style of clothing pictured, can also be clues to era. Some cards are found with copyright dates, but that just tells us when the copyright was given. The card companies often kept the same cards in their lines for many years. These dates are found on many cards from the 1940s, but most later cards were marked with just "copyright." Many cards were hand dated by either the sender or the recipient of the cards. This does tell us when the card was sent, but it could have been in a box of cards somewhere in a drawer for years. The same can be said of those in envelopes with postmarks. If you add up all the information the clues give, you will have a close idea of when the card was made.

Dates in this book are given if the card was marked either by copyright, hand dated, or postmarked. The letters by the date tell us where the information comes from.

c. = copyright
HD = hand dated
PM = postmarked

Storage boxes and pages are available that are archival safe and will protect your collection. Keep your cards away from extreme temperatures, smoke, and moisture.

Be careful with envelopes; the glue can stain the paper as well as the card that is against it. With just a little care, the wonderful pieces of the past that are your cards will be here for many years and future generations to enjoy.

The thrill of the hunt is what keeps most collectors going. Whether you are looking for any and all cards with a certain topic or just trying to hunt down one last card in a series or to complete a boxed set, it's that thrill of finally finding the perfect card that makes collecting one of the most popular pastimes ever.

Babies

For many of us, our greeting card collection started the day we were born. Birth announcements were proudly sent out to friends and family. Congratulations and Welcome Baby cards were received. These cards were lovingly tucked away in a baby book, an album, or a drawer, as a reminder of that special event. Hopefully someone saved them for you and you now have a wonderful sentimental start to your card collection. The cards pictured here are just a sampling of the wonderful baby cards to be found by today's collector.

Welcome, Baby!

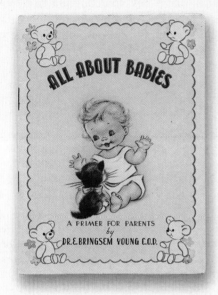

All About Babies by Dr. E. Bringsem Young, c. 1941, 5¾" x 4¾", 14-page primer for parents. Marked: Rust Craft. $3.00 – 10.00.

The ABC's of Babyhood, 5¾" x 4¾", 6-page alphabet definitions. $3.00 – 10.00.

Congratulations

New Baby, HD 1953, 6" x 4¾". Ribbon attachment, four-page fold-out. Marked: Fairfield. $5.00 – 12.00.

To All, 1930s, 5" x 4", attachments of ribbon and lace, parchment. $3.00 – 8.00.

How Happy, 5¼" x 4¼". Marked: Norcross. $3.00 – 10.00.

Lucky Baby, 5¼" x 4¼", embossed. Marked: Hallmark. $3.00 – 8.00.

New Baby, HD 1948. 5¾" x 4¾", padded satin blanket. $3.00 – 8.00.

First Baby, HD 1949, 5¼" x 4½". Marked: Hallmark. $3.00 – 8.00.

Best Wishes, 5¾" x 4¾", embossed. $3.00 – 8.00.

Welcome to Baby, HD 1953, 5¾" x 4½", embossed. Marked: Fairfield. $3.00 – 10.00.

All 'Round, HD 1954, 5" x 4½", embossed, ribbon attachment. Marked: National Printing Co. $3.00 – 8.00.

It's a Girl

Best Wishes, HD 1949, 5¾" x 4¾", embossed,
cord attachment. $3.00 – 8.00.

Baby Girl, c. 1948, 5¾" x 4¾", attached net. Marked:
Rust Craft. $3.00 – 8.00.

New Little Daughter, 6½" x 4", one-sided, on
heavy card card stock. $3.00 – 8.00.

Baby Girl, 7¼" x 3¼", embossed.
Marked: Hallmark. $2.00 – 5.00.

Nothing Sweeter, 4¾" x 4¾", flocked. Marked: Hallmark. $3.00 – 8.00.

Best Wishes, c. 1950, 4" x 5". Marked: Rust Craft. $2.00 – 4.00.

It's a Boy

How Wonderful, 5½" x 4¼", ribbon bow attachment. Marked: Gibson. $2.00 – 5.00.

Nothing Finer, HD 1950, 5½" x 4½", flocked. Marked: Hallmark. $3.00 – 8.00.

Congratulations, 5¾" x 4½", embossed. $2.00 – 5.00.

New Baby, 4½" x 4½". Marked: Hallmark. $2.00 – 5.00.

Congratulations, 5¼" x 4", embossed. Marked: Hallmark. $2.00 – 5.00.

A Baby Boy, HD 1950, 5½" x 4½". Marked: Volland. $2.00 – 5.00.

Babies

To Greet, 5¼" x 4½", flocked blanket. Marked: Norcross. $3.00 – 8.00.

Congratulations, 5¾" x 4¾", novel fold. Marked: Wallace Brown. $3.00 – 8.00.

Happy Trio, 5¾" x 4¾", pop-up. Marked: Wallace Brown. $3.00 – 8.00.

Congratulations, 5¼" x 4¼". Marked: Hallmark. $3.00 – 5.00.

Night Shift, 5¾" x 4½". $3.00 – 5.00.

Congratulations, HD 1950, 5" x 6", pop-up from boxed set Comics on Parade. $3.00 – 8.00.

Baby's First

New Father, 5¼" x 4", pop-up. Marked: Hallmark. $3.00 – 8.00.

Valentine's, c. 1948, 9½" x 7½", 3-D stand-up. Marked: Rust Craft. $5.00 – 15.00.

Valentine's, c. 1952, 6" x 4", embossed. Marked: Rust Craft. $3.00 – 8.00.

Valentine's, HD 1945, 6" x 4¼". Marked: Gibson. $3.00 – 8.00.

Easter, HD 1950, 5½" x 4¼", novel fold. Marked: Gibson. $3.00 – 8.00.

Valentine's, HD 1951, 4½" x 4¾", flocked. Marked: Hallmark. $3.00 – 8.00.

Christmas, HD 1950, 6¾" x 4¼". Marked: Volland. $3.00 – 8.00.

Christmas, c. 1949, 6" x 4". Marked: Rust Craft. $3.00 – 8.00.

Birthdays

Age 1, 5¼" x 4¼", gold trim. Marked:
Made in England. $3.00 – 8.00.

Age 1, 6" x 4", mechanical. Marked:
Norcross. $5.00 – 20.00.

Age 1, 3" x 5", one-sided. $3.00 –
8.00.

Age 1, HD 1943, 5¾" x 4¾", feather attachment.
Marked: Quality Cards. $3.00 – 8.00.

Age 1, 6" x 4". $3.00 – 8.00.

15

Age 1, c. 1950, 6" x 4¾", mechanical. Feet walk when wheel is turned. Marked: Greetings Inc. $3.00 – 8.00.

Age 1, 6" x 4¼". Marked: Gibson. $3.00 – 8.00.

Age 1, 5¼" x 4¼", came with ribbon attachment. Marked: Buzza. $3.00 – 6.00.

Age 1, HD 1946, 6" x 4¼". Marked: Gibson. $3.00 – 8.00.

Age 1, HD 1951, 5½" x 4¼", flocked. Marked:
Gibson. $3.00 – 8.00.

Age 1, c. 1944, 5¾" x 4", granules and flocking.
Marked: Hallmark. $3.00 – 8.00.

Age 1, 4½" x 4½". $3.00 – 6.00.

Age 1, 5¾" x 3¾". $3.00 – 8.00.

Age 2, 5¼" x 4¼", multifold. Marked: Hallmark.
$4.00 – 10.00.

Age 2, 6" x 5", unfolds to be worn as party hat. Marked:
Forget-Me-Not. $3.00 – 8.00.

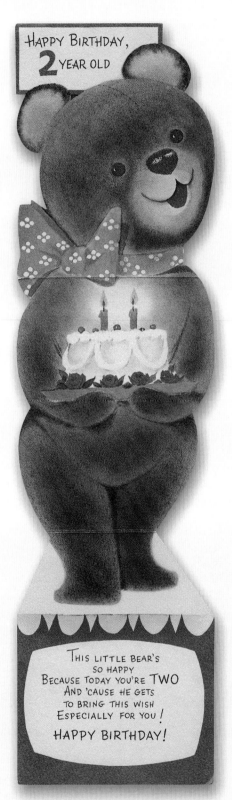

Age 2, open view of bear
at top left, 16" x 4¼".

Age 2, HD 1952, 5" x 6", multifold, stand-up. Marked: Paramount. $4.00 – 10.00.

Age 2, open view of card on left, 10" x 11".

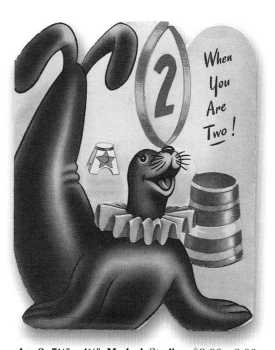

Age 2, 5½" x 4½". Marked: Sterling. $3.00 – 8.00.

Age 2, 7" x 5", attached eyes.
Marked: Hallmark. $3.00 – 8.00.

Age 2, 5¼" x 4½", flocked. Marked:
Norcross. $3.00 – 8.00.

Age 2, 5½" x 4¼", flocked. Marked:
Gibson. $3.00 – 8.00.

Age 2, 5¾" x 4¾", embossed. Marked:
Harmony. $3.00 – 8.00.

Age 2, HD 1943, 6" x 4¼", feather
attachment. Marked: Gibson. $3.00 –
6.00.

Age 2, HD 1956, 5¼" x 4½", flocked number. Marked: Art Guild of Williamsburg.
$3.00 – 8.00.

Age 2, 6" x 5¼". Marked: Art Guild of
Williamsburg. $3.00 – 8.00.

Age 2, HD 1951, 5¾" x 4¾", flocked.
Marked: Forget-Me-Not. $3.00 – 8.00.

Age 2, 4¾" x 4½", flocked. Marked: Hallmark. $3.00 – 8.00.

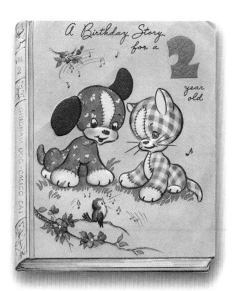

Age 2, c. 1948, 5¾" x 4¾", embossed,
pop-up. Marked: Greetings Inc. $3.00 –
10.00.

Age 2, c. 1945, 5¼" x 4½". Marked: Rust
Craft. $3.00 – 6.00.

Age 3, 5¼" x 3¾". Marked: Hallmark.
$3.00 – 8.00.

Age 3, HD 1945, 5½" x 4½", embossed.
Marked: Merchant. $3.00 – 8.00.

Age 3, HD 1948, 5¼" x 4¼". $3.00 –
5.00.

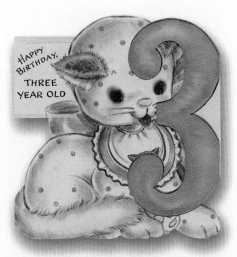

Age 3, 4½" x 4½". Marked: Hallmark.
$3.00 – 8.00.

Age 3, 4½," x 4½", flocked. Marked: Hallmark. $3.00 – 8.00.

Age 3, HD 1945, 4¾" x 4¾". $3.00 – 5.00.

Age 3, 5¼" x 4". $3.00 – 8.00.

Age 3, 5¼" x 4½", flocked. **Marked:** Norcross. $3.00 – 8.00.

Age 3, 4" x 3¾". **Marked:** Gibson. $3.00 – 6.00.

Age 3, 5" x 4". **Marked:** Volland. $3.00 – 8.00.

Age 3, 5¼" x 4¼". $3.00 – 6.00.

Age 3, HD 1945, 5¾" x 4¾", feather attachment. Marked: Quality. $3.00 – 8.00.

Age 3, HD 1950, 6" x 5", embossed textured background. Marked: Art Guild of Williamsburg. $3.00 – 8.00.

Age 3, HD 1953, 5½" x 4½". Marked: Forget-Me-Not. $3.00 – 6.00.

Age 3, c. 1946, 5" x 4¾", pop-up, unfolds into a hat. Marked: Rust Craft. $3.00 – 6.00.

Age 3, HD 1941, 5¼" x 4", attached "3." $3.00 – 6.00.

Age 3, HD 1957, 5½" x 4¾". **Marked: The DA Line.** $3.00 – 8.00.

Age 3, HD 1945, 5¾" x 4¾". $3.00 – 8.00.

Age 4, HD 1954, 6" x 5", book shape. $3.00 – 8.00.

Age 4, HD 1949, 5½" x 4¼", google-eye attachment. $3.00 – 8.00.

Age 4, HD 1952, 5½" x 4½".
Marked: Sterling. $3.00 –
8.00.

Age 4, c. 1945, 6" x 5".
Marked: Greetings Inc.
$3.00 – 8.00.

Age 4, HD 1949, 4¼"' x 5½", has slot for
coins. **Marked:** Gibson. $3.00 – 8.00.

Age 4, 6" x 4¼", folds out. **Marked:**
Mervle. $3.00 – 6.00.

Age 4, 6" x 5", flocked. **Marked:** H.A.C.O.
$3.00 – 8.00.

Age 4, 5½" x 4½". $3.00 – 8.00.

Age 4, 6" x 4", removable baby in pouch. **Marked:** Stanley. $3.00 – 8.00.

Age 4, HD 1952, 5¾" x 4½", pop-up. **Marked:** A Barker Card. $3.00 – 8.00.

Age 4, HD 1954, 5½" x 4¾", glitter trim. $3.00 – 8.00.

Age 4, c. 1952, 5½" x 4½", printed front and back. **Marked:** Greetings Inc. $3.00 – 8.00.

Age 5, 6" x 5". $3.00 – 10.00.

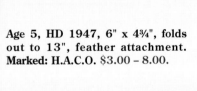

Age 5, c. 1945, 6" x 4", number five of a number-shape series. Marked: Hallmark. $3.00 – 8.00.

Age 5, HD 1947, 6" x 4¾", folds out to 13", feather attachment. Marked: H.A.C.O. $3.00 – 8.00.

Age 5, HD 1950, 6" x 4¼". Marked: Gibson. $3.00 – 8.00.

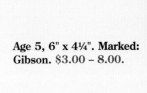

Age 5, 6" x 4¼". Marked: Gibson. $3.00 – 8.00.

Age 5, HD 1946, 6" x 4½", mechanical wheels turn. **Marked:** Gibson (Circus age set). $3.00 – 8.00.

Age 5, HD 1967, 6½" x 4½", embossed. **Marked:** American Greetings. $3.00 – 8.00.

Age 5, 5½" x 4½". **Marked:** Forget-Me-Not. $3.00 – 8.00.

Age 5, HD 1947, 5¾" x 4¾, removable "I Am 5" tag to wear. $3.00 – 8.00.

Age 5, HD 1941, 4¾" x 4". $3.00 – 6.00.

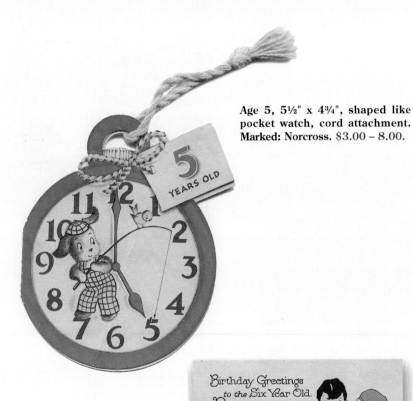

Age 5, 5½" x 4¾", shaped like pocket watch, cord attachment. Marked: Norcross. $3.00 – 8.00.

Age 5, 5¾" x 4¾", embossed. Marked: The DA Line. $3.00 – 8.00.

Age 6, HD 1927, 3½" x 4½", one-sided, heavy card stock. $3.00 – 10.00.

Age 6, HD 1927, 5" x 3¼", folded card stock. $3.00 – 10.00.

Age 6, c. 1952, 5½" x 4½", design printed on front and back. Marked: Greetings Inc. $3.00 – 8.00.

Age 6, 5¾" x 4¼". **Marked: Buzza Cardozo.** $3.00 – 8.00.

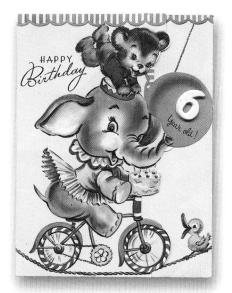

Age 6, 6" x 4¾", embossed, pop-up. **Marked: Sterling.** $3.00 – 8.00.

Age 6, HD 1954, 6" x 5", book shaped. **Marked: Ideal.** $3.00 – 8.00.

Age 6, 5½" x 3½", stand-up. **Marked: Hallmark.** $3.00 – 8.00.

Age 6, HD 1948, 6" x 4¼". **Marked: Gibson.** $3.00 – 8.00.

Age 6, HD 1968, 6" x 4¼". Marked: Greetings Inc. $3.00 – 8.00.

Age 6, c. 1948, 5¾" x 4½", pop-up. Marked: Barker. $3.00 – 8.00.

Age 6, 5½" x 4½". Marked: Sterling. $3.00 – 8.00.

Age 6, c. 1945, 6" x 4", die-cut in the shape of a six, some flocking. Marked: Hallmark. $3.00 – 8.00.

Age 6, 7" x 6", ray gun and arm move. Marked: Munson. $3.00 – 10.00.

Age 7, 6" x 5", embossed. $3.00 – 6.00.

Age 7, c. 1950, 5¾" x 4¾", unique pop-up.
Marked: The DA Line. $3.00 – 10.00.

Age 7, 5½" x 4½", sample card price and
item number stamped on front. Marked: A
Pollyanna Card. $3.00 – 6.00.

Age 7, 5¾" x 4", age sticker applied to
balloon. $3.00 – 8.00.

Age 7, 5" x 6". $3.00 – 8.00.

Age 8, 5" x 4", folds out to 16". Marked: Volland. $3.00 – 8.00.

Age 7, 6" x 5", flocked. Marked: Forget-Me-Not. $3.00 – 8.00.

Age 8, 5¾" x 4½", embossed gold number eight. Marked: Wishing Well Greetings. $3.00 – 8.00.

Age 8, 5¾" x 4¾", flocked. Marked: Forget-Me-Not. $3.00 – 8.00.

Age 8, 5½" x 4½", embossed, sample with price and item number on front. Marked: Sterling. $3.00 – 6.00.

Age 8, 5" x 4¼". $3.00 – 8.00.

Age 8, 5½" x 4½", embossed. $3.00 – 8.00.

Age 9, 5¼" x 4¼". Marked: The Wishing Well. $3.00 – 8.00.

Age 9, 5¼" x 4½". $3.00 – 6.00.

Age 9, 6" x 5", boy pets horse and its eyes move. $3.00 – 10.00.

Age 9, 6" x 4½". Marked: Wishing Well Greetings. $3.00 – 8.00.

Age 9, 6½" x 4¼", flocked sample card with price and item number on front. $3.00 – 6.00.

Age 9, 6¾" x 4½", embossed sample card with price and item number on front. $3.00 – 6.00.

Age 10, 5¾" x 4½", embossed. Marked: Miller Art. $3.00 – 8.00.

Age 10, 6½" x 4¼", embossed, sample with price and item number on front. $3.00 – 8.00.

Age 10, 5¾" x 4¾", flocked. $3.00 – 8.00.

Age 10, HD 1946, 6" x 4½", mechanical. Marked: Gibson (circus age set). $3.00 – 8.00.

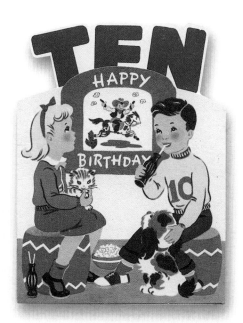

Age 10, 6" x 4½". Marked: Wishing Well Greetings. $3.00 – 8.00.

Age 10, 6" x 4", embossed. $3.00 – 6.00.

Age 11, 5¾" x 4¾", embossed. $3.00 – 8.00.

Age 11, 5¾" x 4½", book shaped. Marked: Wishing Well Greetings. $3.00 – 8.00.

Age 11, 5¾" x 4½", embossed, sample with price and item number on front. $3.00 – 6.00.

Age 11, 6½" x 4¼", embossed. $3.00 – 8.00.

Age 11, 5¾" x 4½", embossed. Marked: Miller Art. $3.00 – 8.00.

Age 11, 5¾" x 4¾", glitter highlights, sample card with price and item number on front. $3.00 – 8.00.

Age 12, 5¾" x 4½", embossed. Marked: Miller Art. $3.00 – 8.00.

Age 12, 5½" x 4½". Marked: Merchant. $3.00 – 8.00.

Age 12, 5¾" x 4½", glitter trim, sample card with price and item number on front. $3.00 – 6.00.

Age 12, 5¾" x 4¾", glitter effect. $3.00 – 8.00.

Age 12, 6" x 4", embossed. $3.00 – 6.00.

Age 12, 5¾" x 4½", embossed, sample card with price and item number on front. $3.00 – 8.00.

English age 3, 5¾" x 7¼", signed "George McKenzie." Marked: Collins greetings cards. $5.00 – 15.00.

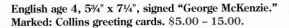

English age 4, 5¾" x 7¼", signed "George McKenzie." Marked: Collins greeting cards. $5.00 – 15.00.

English age 10, 5¾" x 7¼", signed "George McKenzie." Marked: Collins greetings cards. $5.00 – 15.00.

Missed

English, 6" x 4¾". $5.00 – 15.00.

Miscellaneous

English, 6" x 4¾". $5.00 – 15.00.

Girl with Cake, 5¾" x 4", attached felt flower on hat. $3.00 – 8.00.

To a Girl, 5½" x 4½", two cut-out girls on spring jumping rope. Marked: American Greetings. $3.00 – 10.00.

To Nephew, 4½" x 4½". Marked: Hallmark. $3.00 – 8.00.

Boy on Fence, c. 1946, 5½" x 4¼", flocked. $3.00 – 8.00.

To Daughter, c. 1946, 5½" x 4¼", attached cord pulls wagon. $3.00 – 8.00.

Teddy Bear, c. 1942, 6" x 4¾", attached feather. Marked: Hallmark. $3.00 – 8.00.

Girl in Chair, 7" x 3½", embossed. $3.00 – 8.00.

Dear Little Girl, 4¾" x 3¾", signed "J.C. Sax." Marked: Gibson. $3.00 – 8.00.

Sweet Girl, 4¾" x 4¾", sequin jewel collar. Marked: Hallmark. $3.00 – 8.00.

Boy with Wheelbarrow, 6¼" x 4¼". Marked: Gibson. $3.00 – 8.00.

Dog with Ball, c. 1944, 6" x 4", attached feather. Marked: Hallmark. $3.00 – 8.00.

For Niece, 5½" x 3½". Marked: Hallmark. $3.00 – 8.00.

Girl with Cat, HD 1927, 4¾" x 3½", one-sided. Marked: Rust Craft. $3.00 – 10.00.

Children and Flowers, HD 1927, 4¾" x 4", one-sided. Marked: Rust Craft. $3.00 – 10.00.

Boy in Man's Suit Coat, HD 1944, 5¾" x 4¾". $3.00 – 10.00.

Girl and Kittens, HD 1954, 5" x 3½", flocked. Marked: Hallmark. $3.00 – 8.00.

Bears, c. 1947, 4¾" x 4¾", flocked, also found with 1949 copyright and brown flocking. Marked: Hallmark. $3.00 – 8.00.

Little Girl, 5¼" x 4¼". Marked: GB. $3.00 – 6.00.

Bears and Cake, 5" x 6", "happy birthday" folds out into a 30" banner. $3.00 – 8.00.

Girl on Phone, 6" x 4". Marked: Hallmark. $3.00 – 8.00.

To Granddaughter, 4½" x 4¾". Marked: Hallmark.
$3.00 – 8.00.

Children and Dog, 6" x 4", flocked. $3.00 – 8.00.

Girl and Cake, HD 1954, 4½" x 4½", glitter on cake.
Marked: Hallmark. $3.00 – 8.00.

Girl with Basket, c. 1941, 5½" x 4", synthetic
hair. Marked: Hallmark. $3.00 – 8.00.

Characters

Cartoon, Comic, TV, and Movie

Howdy Doody, 4½" x 3½", with Buffalo Bob. Marked: Kagran. $8.00 – 20.00.

Howdy Doody, 4½" x 3½", Phineas T. Bluster inside submarine. Marked: Kagran. $8.00 – 20.00.

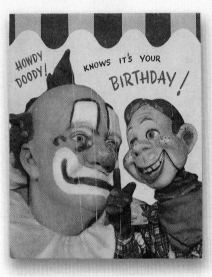

Howdy Doody with Clarabell, 5¾" x 4¾". Marked: Vira Creations. $10.00 – 25.00.

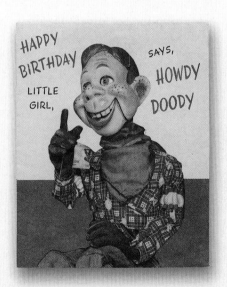

Howdy Doody, 1951, 5¾" x 4¾". Marked: Vira Creations. $10.00 – 25.00.

Popeye, valentine, HD 1948, 4¼" x 4¼", Olive Oyl and Wimpy inside. $5.00 – 35.00.

Popeye, 1929, 4½" x 4¼", "A Valentine fer You." Marked: Hallmark. $5.00 – 35.00.

Felix the Cat, 6" x 4¾", flocked. Marked: Fairbanks. $5.00 – 30.00.

Donald Duck, c. 1941, 5¾" x 4¼", flocked. Marked: Hallmark. $5.00 – 25.00.

Donald Duck, c. 1946, 5" x 5", pop-up. Marked: Hallmark. $5.00 – 30.00.

Mickey Mouse, get well, c. 1942, 4½" x 4½". Marked: Hallmark. $10.00 – 35.00.

Mickey Mouse, HD 1935, 4¾" x 3¾". Marked: Hallmark. $10.00 – 35.00.

Davy Crockett, 5¼" x 4½", fuzzy tail on coonskin hat. Marked: Norcross. $5.00 – 15.00.

Dagwood, c. 1945, 4¾" x 4¾", with ribbon bow tie. Marked: Hallmark. $5.00 – 25.00.

Dagwood and Family, c. 1951, 6" x 5", at Christmas dinner, by Chic Young. Marked: King Features Syndicate Inc. $5.00 – 15.00.

Buz Sawyer, c. 1951, 6" x 5", Christmas greeting by Roy Crane. Marked: King Features Syndicate Inc. $5.00 – 15.00.

Mandrake the Magician, Christmas, c. 1951, 6" x 5". Marked: King Features Syndicate Inc. $5.00 – 15.00.

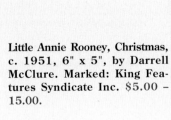

Little Annie Rooney, Christmas, c. 1951, 6" x 5", by Darrell McClure. Marked: King Features Syndicate Inc. $5.00 – 15.00.

Little Iodine, c. 1951, 6" x 5", by Jimmy Hatlo. Marked: King Features Syndicate Inc. $5.00 – 15.00.

Fritz and Hans, Christmas, c. 1951, 6" x 5". Marked: King Features Syndicate Inc. $5.00 – 15.00.

King, Christmas, c. 1951, 6" x 5", by O. Soglow. Marked: King Features Syndicate Inc. $5.00 – 15.00.

Prince Valiant, Christmas, c. 1951, 6" x 5", by H. Foster. Marked: King Features Syndicate Inc. $5.00 – 15.00.

Myrtle, Christmas, c. 1951, 6" x 5", by Dudley Fisher. Marked: King Features Syndicate Inc. $5.00 – 15.00.

Lanky Lil, birthday, HD 1946, 5" x 5".
Marked: Norcross. $5.00 – 15.00.

Lanky Lil, valentine, 11¼" x 6½". $5.00 – 20.00.

Susie Q, Christmas, 4½" x 3½". Marked:
Norcross. $5.00 – 10.00.

Susie Q, Christmas, 4½" x 3½". Marked:
Norcross. $5.00 – 10.00.

Susie Q, valentine, 5" x 4". Marked: Norcross. $5.00 – 15.00.

Logo on back of Susie Q pop-up valentine.

Susie Q, Easter, HD 1944, 5½" x 4½".
Marked: Norcross. $5.00 – 15.00.

Susie Q, valentine, 5½" x 4½", pop-up.
Marked: Norcross. $5.00 – 18.00.

Campbell's Kids

Girl in Swing, birthday, 1978, 7½" x
4½", embossed. Marked: Norcross.
$4.00 – 8.00.

Two Children, 1978, 7½" x 4½",
embossed love notes. Marked: Norcross. $4.00 – 8.00.

Girl and Letter, 1978, 7½" x 4½",
embossed friendship card. Marked:
Norcross. $4.00 – 8.00.

Boy and Pot, 1978, 7½" x 4½", embossed friendship card. Marked: Norcross. $4.00 – 8.00.

Girl and Picnic Basket, birthday, 1978, 7½" x 4½", and embossed. Marked: Norcross. $4.00 – 8.00.

Child Driving Soup Can, birthday, 1978, 7½" x 4½", and embossed. Marked: Norcross. $4.00 – 8.00.

Girl in Ladle, birthday, 1978, 7½" x 4½", embossed. Marked: Norcross. $4.00 – 8.00.

Girl beside Bowl, 1978, 7½" x 4½", embossed love card. Marked: Norcross. $4.00 – 8.00.

Girl with Slate, 1978, 7½" x 4½", embossed friendship card. Marked: Norcross. $4.00 – 8.00.

Girl with Can, birthday, 1978, 7½" x 4½", embossed. Marked: Norcross. $4.00 – 8.00.

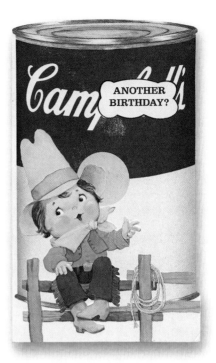

Boy on Fence, 1978, 7½" x 4½", embossed. Marked: Norcross. $4.00 – 8.00.

Children Picnicking, 1978, 7½" x 4½", embossed love card. Marked: Norcross. $4.00 – 8.00.

Child in Costume, 1978, 7½" x 4½", embossed friendship card. Marked: Norcross. $4.00 – 8.00.

Country Life

Down on the Farm

Barn, c. 1936, 5" x 5", fold-out 3-D effect.
Marked: Hallmark. $3.00 – 10.00.

Country Boy, HD 1960, 5" x 4".
Marked: Hallmark. $3.00 – 5.00.

Boy with Duckling, c. 1947, 5" x
3¼", boy is watering the duck.
Marked: Hallmark. $3.00 – 8.00.

Children with Chicks, HD 1945, 5" x 4¼".
Marked: Norcross. $3.00 – 8.00.

Colt, 6" x 3¼". Marked: Gibson.
$3.00 – 6.00.

Child and Puppies, HD 1959,
6¾" x 3", flocked. Marked:
Hallmark. $3.00 – 8.00.

Children and Colt, 5" x 4". $3.00 – 8.00.

Boy and Pup, 5¾" x 5", attached flower. Marked: Gatto. $3.00 – 8.00.

Child with Basket, 4½" x 3½", folds to stand up. $3.00 – 6.00.

Child Pitching Hay, 4½" x 4½". Marked: Hallmark. $3.00 – 6.00.

Calf with Basket, 4¾" x 3¾", signed "J.C. Sax." Marked: Gibson. $3.00 – 8.00.

Child with Ducks, 4½" x 3¾". Marked: Gibson. $3.00 – 8.00.

Boy and Dog, **7" x 3¾"**, dog folds for 3-D effect. Marked: C CO. $3.00 – 8.00.

Girl and Kittens, HD 1945, 5¼" x 4¼". $3.00 – 8.00.

Girl and Boy, 6" x 4¾", novel fold, opens to 14¼". $3.00 – 8.00.

Calf, c. 1945, 4½" x 4". Marked: Hallmark. $3.00 – 8.00.

Boy and Puppy, 5½" x 4½". Marked: Sterling. $3.00 – 8.00.

Girl and Boy, 5¼" x 4¼". $3.00 – 6.00.

Animals

Bunny, 5¾" x 4¾". Marked: Sterling. $3.00 – 8.00.

Bunny, 8¾" x 7", one-sided. Marked: Forget-Me-Not. $5.00 – 15.00.

Bunny, HD 1950, 4¾" x 4½", flocked. Marked: Hallmark. $3.00 – 8.00.

Bunny, 5¾" x 4", flocked. Marked: Hallmark. $3.00 – 8.00.

Bunny, 5¾" x 4¾". Marked: Forget-Me-Not. $3.00 – 8.00.

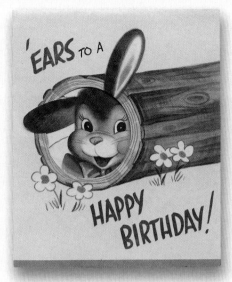

Bunny, 6" x 5", pop-up. $3.00 – 10.00.

Bunny, 6¼" x 4¾", train on wheel that turns. Marked: Sterling. $3.00 – 8.00.

Bunny, 6" x 4", flocked. Marked: Norcross. $3.00 – 8.00.

Bunny, 6" x 4", flocked. Marked: Rust Craft. $3.00 – 8.00.

Duck, HD 1944, 5½" x 4¼". $3.00 – 8.00.

Duck, c. 1946, 4½" x 3½". Marked: Hallmark. $3.00 – 8.00.

Duck, HD 1945, 6" x 4". Marked: Stanley.
$3.00 – 8.00.

Duck, HD 1953, 6" x 4", feather attached.
Marked: Paramount. $3.00 – 8.00.

Duck, 6" x 4", flocked. Marked: Hallmark. $3.00 – 8.00.

Duck, 5½" x 4¼".
$3.00 – 8.00.

Duck, HD 1952, 6" x 4", flocked. Marked:
Hallmark. $3.00 – 8.00.

Duck, 4½" x 4¾". Marked:
Hallmark. $3.00 – 8.00.

Duck, HD 1948, 5½" x 4¼", attached pop-up feather. Marked: Gibson. $3.00 – 8.00.

Duck, c. 1947, 6" x 4", flocked. Marked: Hallmark. $3.00 – 8.00.

Duck, HD 1957, 6½" x 3¼", glitter. Marked: Gibson. $3.00 – 8.00.

Duck, c. 1949, 5¼" x 4½", printed front and back. Marked: Hallmark. $3.00 – 8.00.

Cowboys and Indians

Coach and Horses, HD 1970, 6¾" x 4½". Marked: Hallmark. $4.00 – 8.00.

Cowboy and Cowgirl, HD 1948, 6" x 5". $3.00 – 8.00.

Cowboy and Cowgirl, 6" x 4¾". Marked: Hampton Art. $3.00 – 8.00.

Cowboy with Lasso, HD 1952, 6" x 4", flocked. Marked: Rust Craft. $3.00 – 8.00.

Cowboy and Cowgirl, 6" x 4". Marked: Paramount. $3.00 – 8.00.

Cowboy on Horse, HD 1951, 4½" x 4½". Marked: Hallmark. $3.00 – 8.00.

Cowboy with Lasso, 6" x 4½", gun can be removed from holster. Marked: Wishing Well Greetings. $3.00 – 8.00.

Cowboy on Fence, 6" x 4", glitter. Marked: Rust Craft. $3.00 – 8.00.

Cowboy on Horse, 5½" x 4½", glitter. Marked: Art Guild of Williamsburg. $3.00 – 6.00.

Cowboy and Cowgirl, 5½" x 4¼", flocked, signed "Myers." Marked: Gibson. $3.00 – 8.00.

Cowboy on Horse, 8" x 4", flocked. Marked: Gibson. $3.00 – 8.00.

Cowboy and Horse, 4¾" x 4¾". $3.00 – 6.00.

Six-shooter, 4¾" x 4¾", removable gun. Marked: Doehla fine arts. $3.00 – 8.00.

Cowboy and Horse, HD 1952, 6" x 4", flocked. Marked: Rust Craft. $3.00 – 8.00.

Little Sheriff, 6¼" x 4½", embossed. Marked: Hallmark. $3.00 – 8.00.

Cowboy with Guitar, 5½" x 4¼". Marked: Hallmark. $3.00 – 8.00.

Cowgirl, 6½" x 3½", flocked background. Marked: Volland. $3.00 – 8.00.

Cowboy with Guitar, 6" x 4", glitter on guitar. Marked: Hallmark. $3.00 – 8.00.

Cowboy and Cowgirl, 5½" x 4½", embossed. $3.00 – 8.00.

Cowboy and Cowgirl, HD 1953, 6" x 5", pop-up, flocked. Marked: The DA Line. $3.00 – 10.00.

Cowboy Singing, HD 1959, 7¼" x 3", glitter trim. Marked: Hallmark. $3.00 – 8.00.

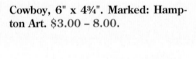

Cowboy, 6" x 4¾". Marked: Hampton Art. $3.00 – 8.00.

Cowboy on Rocking Horse, 6" x 4¾", one-sided, tabs fold to allow it to stand up. $3.00 – 8.00.

Cowboy, 5" x 4¾", glitter trim. Marked: Rust Craft. $3.00 – 8.00.

Pinto, HD 1951, 4¾" x 4½", flocked.
Marked: Hallmark. $3.00 – 8.00.

Indian, HD 1959, 6" x 4", glitter.
Marked: Rust Craft. $3.00 – 8.00.

Indian, 6" x 4". Marked: A Sunshine
Card. $3.00 – 8.00.

Children Dressed as Indians, 6½" x
4½", pop-up. Marked: Greetings
Inc. $3.00 – 8.00.

Indians and Teepee, 7" x 4".
Marked: Dreyfuss. $3.00 – 8.00.

Child Playing Indian, 7" x
3¾". Marked: Hallmark Slim
Jims. $3.00 – 8.00.

Indian, HD 1951, 5½" x 4¼".
Marked: Gibson. $3.00 – 8.00.

Indian and Teepee, c. 1950, 6" x 5", embossed, feather attachment. Marked: Greetings Inc. $3.00 – 8.00.

Indian in Headdress, 3¾" x 3", single-sided. $3.00 – 5.00.

Totem Pole, HD 1959, 7¼" x 3¼". Marked: Forget-Me-Not. $2.00 – 4.00.

Indian Running, 7" x 5", dot-to-dot puzzle inside. $3.00 – 8.00.

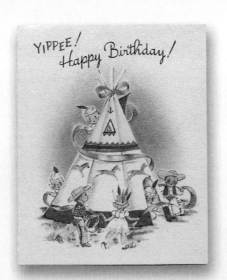

Teepee, HD 1951, 5" x 4¼". Marked: Buzza Cardozo. $3.00 – 5.00.

Indians, c. 1941, 5" x 5". Marked: Hallmark. $3.00 – 8.00.

Hallmark Dolls from the Land of Make Believe

This set included 16 different cards. Each card was decorated with a feather and a sequin jewel. The back of each card is the back of doll. Cards were made of sturdy card stock so they could be stood up for display. Each card was 5½" x 7" and was manufactured by Hall Brothers, Inc.

Front view of Little Bo Peep, c. 1947, printed front and back, feather and sequin attached. Marked: Hallmark. $8.00 – 45.00.

Back view of Little Bo Peep.

Inside view of Little Bo Peep.

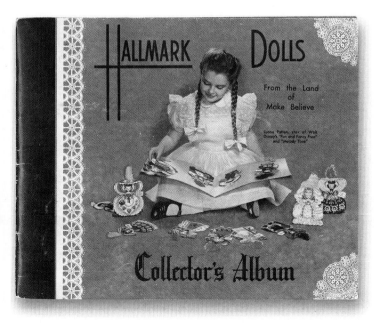

Hallmark Dolls from the Land of Make Believe album, c. 1948, for storing your collection of doll cards. Cover features Luana Patten, star of Walt Disney's *Fun and Fancy Free* and *Melody Time*. $20.00 – 45.00.

THEY'RE BACK!

Straight from the land

This Hallmark Collector's Album makes it easy for a little girl to start a collection of all 16 Hallmark Dolls from the Land of Make-Believe. Buy the album with the first doll; then add to her collection from time to time. She can take them out to play with — put them back to keep them looking fresh as new. And the price is only 50c.

Hallmark From the Land of Make Believe cards and album two-page magazine advertisment, 1954, 14" x 10¼". Note that the album has changed since the 1948 edition shown on page 67. $5.00 – 15.00.

# of Make Believe

LITTLE
RED RIDING
HOOD

Little
Bo-Peep

Cinderella

Every little girl will want a set of these enchanting Hallmark Dolls

Cinderella, Peter Piper, Little Bo Peep, Little Miss Muffet—these story-book
friends, 16 in all, can now become playmates for your favorite little girl.
    For these Hallmark Dolls look as though they stepped right out of fairyland
in all their glory . . . resplendent with real plumes and sparkling sequins.

And inside each card is the fairy tale of the doll. It's written in rhyme
in such an interesting way that youngsters will relive the story again and again
—also its moral and the lesson it teaches. So today, send that little girl
a Hallmark Doll from the Land of Make-Believe. Your choice of dolls
just 25c with envelope—in the stores where Hallmark Cards are sold.

P.S. See Hallmark Dress-Up Dolls, too—with complete wardrobes of punch-out
dresses, hats and pocketbooks. Four different sets—25c each, with envelope.

Hallmark Cards

When you care enough to send the very best

#2 Cinderella, c. 1947. Marked: Hallmark.
$8.00 – 45.00.

#3 Mary Quite Contrary, c. 1947. Marked:
Hallmark. $8.00 – 45.00.

#4 Mary Had a Little Lamb, c. 1947.
Marked: Hallmark. $8.00 – 45.00.

#5 Little Red Riding Hood, c. 1947.
Marked: Hallmark. $8.00 – 45.00.

#6 Little Miss Muffet, c. 1947. Marked:
Hallmark. $8.00 – 45.00.

#7 Tommy Tucker, c. 1947. Marked:
Hallmark. $8.00 – 45.00.

#9 My Pretty Maid, c. 1947. Marked: Hallmark. $8.00 – 45.00.

#10 Little Girl with a Little Curl, c. 1947. Marked: Hallmark. $8.00 – 45.00.

#8 Little Boy Blue, c. 1947. Marked: Hallmark. $8.00 – 45.00.

#11 The Queen of Hearts, c. 1947. Marked: Hallmark. $8.00 – 45.00.

#12 Bobby Shaftoe, c. 1947. Marked: Hallmark. $8.00 – 45.00.

#13 Little Polly Flinders, c. 1947. Marked: Hallmark. $8.00 – 45.00.

#16 Peter Piper, c. 1947. Marked: Hallmark. $8.00 – 45.00.

#14 Curly Locks, c. 1947. Marked: Hallmark. $8.00 – 45.00.

#15 Polly Put the Kettle On, c. 1947. Marked: Hallmark. $8.00 – 45.00.

Hallmark Dolls of the Nations

Hallmark's second series of doll cards was introduced in 1948 with the first eight cards in the Dolls of the Nations series. The remaining eight dolls in the set were released the next year. Cards were 5½" x 7" tall.

Dolls of the Nations album, c. 1948. 10¼" x 13". Marked: Hallmark. $20.00 – 45.00.

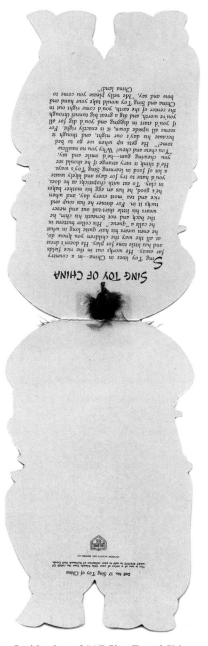

#17 Sing Toy of China, c. 1948. Marked: Hallmark. $8.00 – 45.00.

Back view of #17 Sing Toy of China.

Sing Toy lives in China—in a country far away. He works out in the rice fields and has little time for play. He doesn't dress at all the way the children you know do, he even wears his hair quite long in what he calls a "queue." His collar buttons in the back and not beneath his chin, he wears his little shirt-tail out and never tucks it in. For dinner he has soup and rice and tea most every day, and when he's good, he has an egg his mother bakes in clay. To eat with chopsticks as he does, you'd have to try for days and likely waste a lot of food in learning Sing Toy's ways. He'd think it very strange if he should see you chewing gum—he'd smile and say, "Why you no swallow some?" He gets up when we go to bed because his day's our night, and though it seems all upside down, it is exactly right. For if you'd start in digging and you'd dig for all you're worth, and dig a great big tunnel through the center of the earth, you'd come right out in China and Sing Toy would take your hand and bow and say, "Me velly please you come to China land!"

Sing Toy of China

Doll No. 17 Sing Toy of China

This is one of a series of your little friends from the LAND OF MAKE BELIEVE. Be sure to add all to your collection of Hallmark Doll Cards.

COPYRIGHT HALLMARK INC, KANSAS CITY, MO.

Inside view of #17 Sing Toy of China.

#18 Maria from Mexico, c. 1948. Marked: Hallmark. $8.00 – 45.00.

#19 Antoninette of France. 8.00 – 30.00.

#20 Rita from Brazil, c. 1948. Marked: Hallmark. $8.00 – 45.00.

#21 Katrinka of Holland, c. 1948. Marked: Hallmark. $8.00 – 45.00.

#22 John, a Royal Canadian Mountie, c. 1948. Marked: Hallmark. $8.00 – 45.00.

#23 Cowboy Joe, c. 1948. Marked: Hallmark. $8.00 – 45.00.

#24 Ann of England, c. 1948. Marked: Hallmark. $8.00 – 45.00.

#25 Kathleen of Ireland, c. 1949. Marked: Hallmark. $8.00 – 45.00.

#26 Tautuk of Alaska, c. 1949.
Marked: Hallmark. $8.00 – 45.00.

#27 Christina of Sweden, c. 1949. Marked:
Hallmark. $8.00 – 45.00.

#28 Leilani of Hawaii, c. 1949.
Marked: Hallmark. $8.00 – 45.00.

#29 Monty of Australia, c. 1949.
Marked: Hallmark. $8.00 – 45.00.

#30 Barbel of Switzerland, c. 1949.
Marked: Hallmark. $8.00 – 45.00.

#31 Sandy of Scotland, c. 1949.
Marked: Hallmark. $8.00 – 45.00.

#32 Kusum of India, c. 1949.
Marked: Hallmark. $8.00 – 45.00.

Little Women

The third and final set in the Hallmark doll card series was the Little Women set, and it proved to be the most successful of all. During the filming of the movie *Little Women*, Hallmark artist Vivian Trillow Smith went to the MGM studio and sketched the stars in their costumes. It was from these sketches and photos that she designed the cards with such authentic detail. Inside each card is a description of the character and the signature of the actress who played her. June Allison played Jo, Janet Leigh played Meg, Margaret O'Brien played Beth, and Elizabeth Taylor played Amy. Hallmark timed the first ads for this series with the release of the movie. These cards were a tremendous success and are now some of the most sought after by card collectors.

Little Women set cover, c. 1949, 9" x 5½".
Marked: Hallmark. $10.00 – $15.00.

Janet Leigh as Meg, feather and jewel, c. 1949, 6" x 5". Marked: Hallmark. $30.00 – 75.00 each.

Back view of Meg.

Inside view of Meg.

June Allyson as Jo, c. 1949, 6" x 5". Marked: Hallmark. $30.00 – 75.00 each.

Elizabeth Taylor as Amy, c. 1949, 6" x 5". Marked: Hallmark. $30.00 – 75.00 each.

Margaret O' Brien as Beth, c. 1949, 6" x 5". Marked: Hallmark. $30.00 – 75.00 each.

American Greetings Storyland Doll Cards

The Storyland doll cards are very similar to the earlier Hallmark sets. Each card is printed on both front and back and had a removable tag to be signed by the sender. Inside, a story or nursery rhyme is printed. The cards were sold as individual cards or as a boxed set. The boxed cards all had feathers on the hats, while the cards sold separately did not.

Goldilocks, c. 1949, 6" x 5". Marked: American Greetings. $8.00 – 18.00.

Box for set of Storybook Dolls, c. 1949, 6" x 5". Marked: American Greetings. $6.00 – 10.00.

Back view of Goldilocks.

Inside view of Goldilocks.

GOLDILOCKS

THIS LITTLE GIRL'S NAME IS GOLDILOCKS, FOR HER HAIR IS THE COLOR OF GOLD, AND SHE OFTEN GOES OUT FOR A WALK IN THE WOODS TO PICK PRETTY FLOWERS, I'M TOLD. ONE DAY, WHILE OUT WALKING, SHE HAPPENED TO SEE A CUTE LITTLE VINE-COVERED HOUSE, AND SINCE NO ONE WAS HOME SHE JUST OPENED THE DOOR AND TIPTOED IN, STILL AS A MOUSE. INSIDE SHE DISCOVERED, WERE THREE PORRIDGE BOWLS AND THREE DIFFERENT SIZES OF CHAIRS, AND SHE KNEW RIGHT AWAY THAT THIS COTTAGE MUST BE THE HOME OF THE FAMOUS THREE BEARS. SHE TASTED THE PORRIDGE AND SAT DOWN TO REST, BUT THEN DECIDED INSTEAD, TO CLIMB UP THE STAIRS AND TO LIE DOWN FOR A WHILE, FOR A SHORT NAP ON BABY BEAR'S BED. NOW WHILE SHE WAS SLEEPING THE THREE BEARS CAME HOME, AND THEY BLINKED WHEN THEY ALL CAME INSIDE, FOR BABY BEAR'S BOWL WITH THE PORRIDGE ALL GONE WAS THE VERY FIRST THING THAT THEY SPIED. THEN FATHER BEAR ROARED IN A DEEP, BOOMING VOICE, AND MOTHER SPOKE SOFTLY AND LOW, AND BABY BEAR CRIED IN A HIGH, SQUEAKY VOICE, "SOMEBODY HAS BEEN HERE, I KNOW!" SO THEY HURRIED UPSTAIRS WHERE DEAR GOLDI-LOCKS WAS, AND SHE WOKE UP, AND WHAT DO YOU THINK? WHEN SHE SAW THE THREE BEARS, SHE LET OUT A LOUD CRY AND JUMPED UP AS QUICK AS A WINK. SHE CLIMBED OUT THE WINDOW AND HURRIED FOR HOME, SO FRIGHTENED SHE RAN ALL THE WAY—BUT THE BEARS REALLY LIKED HER, AND ALL OF THEM HOPE THAT SHE'LL COME BACK TO VISIT SOME DAY!

Copyright 1949
American Greeting Publishers, Inc.

Cinderella, c. 1949, 6" x 5". Marked: American Greetings. $8.00 – 18.00.

Curly Locks, c. 1949, 6" x 5". Marked: American Greetings. $8.00 – 18.00.

Little Boy Blue, c. 1949, 6" x 5". Marked: American Greetings. $8.00 – 18.00.

Jack and Jill, c. 1949, 6" x 5". Marked: American Greetings. $8.00 – 18.00.

Mary and Her Little Lamb, c. 1949, 6" x 5". Marked: American Greetings. $8.00 – 18.00.

Queen of Hearts, c. 1949, 6" x 5". Marked: American Greetings. $8.00 – 18.00.

Snow White, c. 1949, 6" x 5". Marked: American Greetings. $8.00 – 18.00.

Little Miss Muffet, c. 1949, 6" x 5". Marked: American Greetings. $8.00 – 18.00.

Little Bo Peep, c. 1949, 6" x 5". Marked: American Greetings. $8.00 – 18.00.

Little Girl with the Curl, c. 1949, 6" x 5". Marked: American Greetings. $8.00 – 18.00.

Little Red Riding Hood, c. 1949, 6" x 5". Marked: American Greetings. $8.00 – 18.00.

International Dolls

China, c. 1949, 6" x 5", printed front and back. Marked: Greetings Inc. $8.00 – 20.00.

Mexico, c. 1949, 6" x 5". Marked: Greetings Inc. $8.00 – 20.00.

Ireland, c. 1949, 6" x 5". Marked: Greetings Inc. $8.00 – 20.00.

Hawaii, c. 1949, 6" x 5". Marked: Greetings Inc. $8.00 – 20.00.

Holland, c. 1949, 6" x 5". Marked: Greetings Inc. $8.00 – 20.00.

Southern Belle, c. 1949, 6" x 5", not marked with country but same style. Marked: Greetings Inc. $8.00 – 20.00.

Nursery Rhyme Dolls

Queen of Hearts, 6" x 5", printed on front and back. Marked: Fairfield. $8.00 – 20.00.

Goldilocks, 6" x 5". Marked: Fairfield. $8.00 – 20.00.

Cinderella, 6" x 5". Marked: Fairfield. $8.00 – 20.00.

Little Miss Muffet, 6" x 5". Marked: Fairfield. $8.00 – 20.00.

Alice in Wonderland, 6" x 5". Marked: Fairfield. $8.00 – 20.00.

Story Book Dolls

Prince Charming, 6" x 5", valentine printed on front and back. Marked: A-Meri-Card. $8.00 – 18.00.

Cinderella, 6" x 5", valentine printed on front and back. Marked: A-Meri-Card. $8.00 – 18.00.

Jack of Hearts, 6" x 5", valentine printed on front and back. Marked: A-Meri-Card. $8.00 – 18.00.

Queen of Hearts, 6" x 5", valentine printed on front and back. Marked: A-Meri-Card. $8.00 – 18.00.

Russian Matryoshka Cards

These cards are patterned after Russian nesting dolls, called Matryoshkas. The dolls nest one inside another till you get to the tiniest center doll. You will find an average of 5 – 10 dolls in a set. With the largest know set made in 1967 by S. Malrutin that consisted of 60 pieces, now on display in a Russian Museum. The brightly colored Matroyoshka Dolls were designed both as a toy and a souvenir, the first thing a tourist sees when visiting Russia are these colorful pieces of art.

The cards pictured here are from 2002 and can still be found in some Russian gift shops online. Available both blank inside or with a Russian saying. Translations are included with the cards.

Beautifully designed, these large, brightly colored cards are printed on both front and back and are wonderful examples of the cards available to today's collector. They are a perfect fit in your doll card collection.

Blond Girl, holding spring flowers, 8¼" x 5", blank. Marked: Made in Russia. $2.00 – 4.00.

Girl, holding summer basket of fruit, 8¼" x 5", blank. Marked: Made in Russia. $2.00 – 4.00.

Girl, holding fall leaves and with basket of apples, 8¼" x 5", blank. Marked: Made in Russia. $2.00 – 4.00.

Girl, wearing winter mittens, 8¼" x 5", blank. Marked: Made in Russia. $2.00 – 4.00.

Girl, holding jar, 8¼" x 5", cat in front, Russian greeting inside. Marked: Made in Russia. $2.00 – 4.00.

Translation: "Enjoy your life and accumulate wealth, celebrate a holiday, treat your guests!"

Old Lady, holding chicken, 8¼" x 5", Russian greeting inside. Marked: Made in Russia. $2.00 – 4.00.

Back of card.

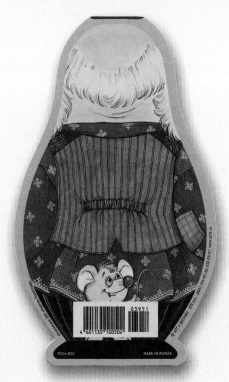

Old Man with Beard, wearing red, 8¼" x 5", Russian greeting inside. Marked: Made in Russia. $2.00 – 4.00.

Back of card.

Girl, holding handkerchief, 8¼" x 5", Russian greeting inside. Marked: Made in Russia. $2.00 – 4.00.

Translation: "Clear skies, Fresh bread, Good friends, All are to live in happiness!"

Dolls with Hair

Christmas, 1920s, 6¾" x 5", one-sided, easel back, synthetic hair attached, hand colored. $10.00 – 35.00.

Christmas, 1920s, 6¾" x 5", one-sided, easel back, synthetic hair attached, hand colored. $10.00 – 35.00.

Birthday, 1920s, 6¾" x 5", one-sided, easel
back, synthetic hair attached, hand colored.
$10.00 – 35.00.

Christmas, 1920s, 6¾" x 5", one-sided, easel
back, synthetic hair attached, hand colored.
$10.00 – 35.00.

Christmas, 1920s, 6¾" x 5", one-sided, easel
back, synthetic hair attached, hand colored.
$10.00 – 35.00.

Birthday, 1920s, 6¾" x 5", one-sided, easel
back, synthetic hair attached, hand colored.
$10.00 – 35.00.

Southern Belles

With Parasol, 6" x 5", inside picture of two more girls in long dresses. $5.00 – 10.00.

For a Niece, HD 1950s, 7" x 5½", real hair, attached tab for standing up to display. Marked: Norcross. $10.00 – 25.00.

With Kittens, 6" x 5", inside picture of two more girls in long dresses, one on back also. Marked: Fairfield. $5.00 – 10.00.

Holding Hat, HD 1949, 5¾" x 4½", inside picture of two more girls in long dresses. Marked: Forget-Me-Not. $5.00 – 10.00.

With Kitten, 5¾" x 5", inside picture of two more girls in long dresses. Marked: Forget–Me–Not. $5.00 – 10.00.

Southern Belles, HD 1950, 6" x 5", inside picture of two more girls in long dresses. Marked: Forget-Me-Not. $3.00 – 8.00.

Inside view of card above right.

Fairy Tales and Nursery Rhymes

Boxed Sets

The American Gretting Card Company produced Little Folks a set of 16 nursery rhyme cards came with either the song or story printed on a four-page insert. These were sold as a boxed set. 6" x 5", 1949, $4.00 – 12.00 each.

1. The Three Little Pigs
2. All Around the Mulberry Bush
3. Ten Little Indians
4. Mary had a Little Lamb
5. Farmer in the Dell
6. Peter Rabbit
7. Old King Cole
8. Jack in the Beanstalk
9. Goldilocks and the Three Bears
10. Billy Boy
11. Little Red Riding Hood
12. The Three Little Kittens
13. Little Boy Blue
14. Little Miss Muffet
15. London Bridge
16. Jack and Jill

Jack and Jill, c. 1949, 6" x 5". Marked: American Greetings.
$4.00 – 12.00.

The Three Little Pigs, c. 1948, 6" x 5". Marked: American
Greetings. $4.00 – 12.00.

Little Miss Muffet, c. 1948, 6" x 5". Marked: American
Greetings. $4.00 – 12.00.

Little Red Riding Hood, c. 1949, 6" x 5". Marked: American
Greetings. $4.00 – 12.00.

Jack and the Beanstalk, c. 1948, 6" x 5". Marked: American Greetings. $4.00 – 12.00.

Goldilocks and the Three Bears, c. 1948, 6" x 5". Marked: American Greetings. $4.00 – 12.00.

The Farmer in the Dell, c. 1948, 6" x 5". Marked: American Greetings. $4.00 – 12.00.

Old King Cole, c. 1948, 6" x 5". Marked: American Greetings. $4.00 – 12.00.

Mary and Her Little Lamb, c. 1948, 6" x 5". Marked: American Greetings. $4.00 – 12.00.

Billy Boy, c. 1948, 6" x 5". Marked: American Greetings. $4.00 – 12.00.

Little Boy Blue, c. 1948, 6" x 5". Marked: American Greetings. $4.00 – 12.00.

Ten Little Indians, c. 1948, 6" x 5". Marked: American Greetings. $4.00 – 12.00.

London Bridge, c. 1948, 6" x 5". Marked: American Greetings. $4.00 – 12.00.

All around the Mulberry Bush, c. 1948, 6" x 5". Marked: American Greetings. $4.00 – 12.00.

Peter Rabbit, c. 1948, 6" x 5". Marked: American Greetings. $4.00 – 12.00.

The Three Little Kittens, c. 1948, 6" x 5". Marked: American Greetings. $4.00 – 12.00.

Little Folks box for cards on preceding page, c. 1948, 6¼" x 5½". Marked: American Greetings. $5.00 – 10.00.

Box for Song and Story Greeting Cards, c. 1950, 6¼" x 5½", each card has insert for song or story, 9 of original 14 shown. Marked: American Greetings. $5.00 – 10.00.

Little Bo-Peep, c. 1950, 6" x 5". Marked: American Greetings. $4.00 – 12.00.

Curly Locks, c. 1950, 6" x 5". Marked: American Greetings. $4.00 – 12.00.

Peter, Peter, Pumpkin-Eater, c. 1950, 6" x 5".
Marked: American Greetings. $4.00 – 12.00.

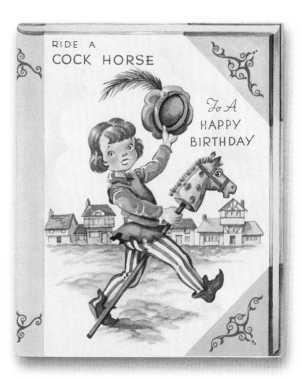

Ride a Cock Horse, c. 1950, 6" x 5". Marked:
American Greetings. $4.00 – 12.00.

Hansel and Gretel, c. 1950, 6" x 5". Marked:
American Greetings. $4.00 – 12.00.

Humpty Dumpty, c. 1950, 6" x 5". Marked: American
Greetings. $4.00 – 12.00.

The Gingerbread Man, c. 1950, 6" x 5". Marked: American Greetings. $4.00 – 12.00.

Tommy Tucker, c. 1950, 6" x 5". Marked: American Greetings. $4.00 – 12.00.

Cinderella, c. 1950, 6" x 5". Marked: American Greetings. $4.00 – 12.00.

Others

Series, The Farmer in the Dell (open view), 6" x 5" (opens to 14½"). $4.00 – 8.00.

Series, The Queen of Hearts, 6" x 5". $4.00 – 8.00.

Series, Simple Simon, 6" x 5". $4.00 – 8.00.

Series, Cinderella, 6" x 5". $4.00 – 8.00.

Series, Hansel and Gretel, 6" x 5". $4.00 – 8.00.

Series, Ol' King Cole, 6" x 5". $4.00 – 8.00.

Mary had a Little Lamb, HD 1953, 6" x 5", novel fold, mechanical (lamb runs by Mary when opened). $5.00 – 10.00.

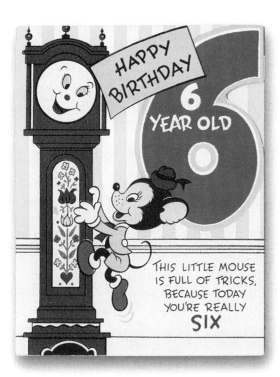

Hickory Dickory Dock, c. 1949, 5¾" x 4½",
mechanical (mouse runs up clock when opened).
Marked: Barker. $5.00 – 10.00.

Hickory Dickory Dock opened.

Old Woman Who Lived in a Shoe, has tiny children to cut out and stand up, 6" x 4½", Marked:
Gartner and Dender Inc. $4.00 – 8.00.

Sing a Song of Six Pence, HD 1952, 6" x 4¾", mechanical (blackbirds fly out of pie when opened). $5.00 – 10.00.

Humpty Dumpty, c. 1949, 5¾" x 4½", mechanical (Humpty Dumpty falls off wall when card is opened). Marked: Barker. $5.00 – 10.00.

Three Little Pigs, 5½" x 4¼", novel fold. Marked: Gibson. $5.00 – 8.00.

Three Little Pigs, 3¾" x 4", cut out. Marked: Hallmark. $4.00 – 8.00.

Get Well

Nurse, 9" x 5½", easel back, hot water bottle attachment opens to reveal greeting. $8.00 – 20.00.

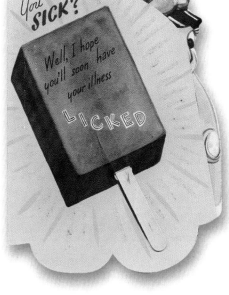

The DA Line, Good Humor delivery truck, 6¼" x 5", with attached stick. $8.00 – 20.00.

Inside view of Good Humor truck.

**Bunny, c. 1947, 6" x 4",
flocked. Marked: Hallmark.
$4.00 – 8.00.**

**Bear, 6½" x 5".
$4.00 – 8.00.**

**Mouse, 6¾" x 4¾", flocked.
$4.00 – 8.00.**

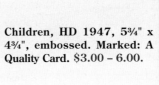

**Ducks, 5¾" x 4½8". Marked:
Forget-Me-Not. $3.00 – 6.00.**

**Children, HD 1947, 5¾" x
4¾", embossed. Marked: A
Quality Card. $3.00 – 6.00.**

Sheep, 6" x 5", flocked. Marked:
H.A.CO. $4.00 – 8.00.

Cat Nurse, 6" x 4".
Marked: Stanley.
$4.00 – 10.00.

5½" x 4¼". Marked: Forget-
Me-Not. $3.00 – 8.00.

Chicks, HD 1959, 5¼" x 4¼", removable pin for the Tonsils Out Club.
Marked: Hallmark. $3.00 – 8.00.

Nurse Blue Bird, 4¾" x 4".
Marked: Stanley. $3.00 – 8.00.

Train, HD 1959, 5½" x 4½", gold-foil "Get Well Soon" sticker, embossed. Marked: Stanley. $3.00 – 8.00.

Puppy, 5" x 4". Marked: Gibson. $3.00 – 6.00.

Puppy in Watering Can, c. 1948, 5¼" x 5½". Marked: Rust Craft. $3.00 – 6.00.

Little Boy, 6½" x 4¼", pop-up opens from center. Marked: H.A.CO. $4.00 – 10.00.

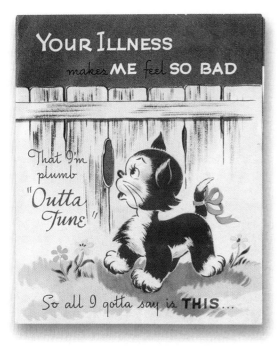

Cat, HD 1942, 5¾" x 4¾", pop-up. Marked: G.E. $4.00 – 8.00.

Kitten Nurse, c. 1942, 5¼" x 4½". Marked: Rust Craft. $3.00 – 6.00.

Child and Dog, HD 1934, 5¼" x 4¼", one-sided, ribbon attachment, puppy pulling on blanket. $4.00 – 8.00.

Puppy, 1930s, 5¾" x 4½", ribbon attachment on pup's neck. $4.00 – 8.00.

107

Gingham Dog, Calico Cat, and Friends

The Duel
(The Gingham Dog and Calico Cat)
by Eugene Field, 1850 – 1895

The gingham dog and the calico cat
Side by side on the table sat;
'Twas half-past twelve, and (what do you think!)
Nor one nor t' other had slept a wink!
The old Dutch clock and the Chinese plate
Appeared to know as sure as fate
There was going to be a terrible spat.
(I wasn't there; I simply state
What was told to me by the Chinese plate!)

The gingham dog went "bow-wow-wow!"
And the calico cat replied "mee-ow!"
The air was littered, an hour or so,
With bits of gingham and calico,
While the old Dutch clock in the chimney-place
Up with its hands before its face,
For it always dreaded a family row!
(Never mind; I'm only telling you
What the old Dutch clock declares is true!)

The Chinese plate looked very blue,
And wailed, "Oh dear! What shall we do!"
But the gingham dog and the calico cat
Wallowed this way and tumbled that,
Employing every tooth and claw
In the awfullest way you ever saw —
And, oh! How the gingham and calico flew!
(Don't fancy I exaggerate —
I got my news from the Chinese plate!)

Next morning where the two had sat
They found no trace of dog or cat;
And some folks think unto this day
That burglar stole that pair away!
But the truth about the cat and pup
Is this: they ate each other up!
Now what do you really think of that!
(The old Dutch clock it told me so,
And that is how I came to know.)

Birthday, 9¼" x 7", large easel back, red and white, for 5 year old. Marked: Forget-Me-Not. $5.00 – 15.00.

Christmas, HD 1945, 5¼" x 4". Marked: Rust Craft. $3.00 – 8.00.

Birthday, HD 1945, 5¾" x 4¾". Marked: American Greetings. $3.00 – 8.00.

Get Well, c. 1940, 6" x 4", cat has whiskers. Marked: Hallmark. $3.00 – 8.00.

Birthday, 6" x 4", pin for 4 year old, attached. Marked: Hallmark. $3.00 – 8.00.

Valentine's Day, HD 1950, 6" x 4".
Marked: Hallmark. $3.00 – 8.00.

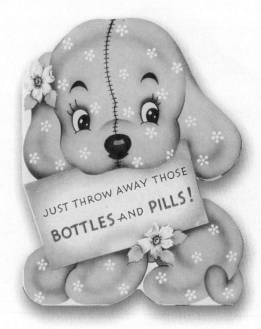

Get Well, 5½" x 4¼". $3.00 – 6.00.

Birthday, 6" x 5". $3.00 – 8.00.

Birthday, 6" x 4¼", red feather attachments. Marked: Gibson. $3.00 – 8.00.

Party invitation, c. 1949, 3" x 4¼". Marked: Rust Craft. $2.00 – 5.00.

Birthday, 5¾" x 4¾". $3.00 – 8.00.

Birthday, HD 1948, 6" x 4", "5" attached. Marked: Stanley. $4.00 – 8.00.

Birthday, 5¼" x 3½", glitter. Marked: Norcross. $3.00 – 6.00.

Get Well, 6½" x 5½". $4.00 – 8.00.

111

Birthday, c. 1945, 5¾" x 4".
Marked: Hallmark. $3.00 –
8.00.

Get Well, c. 1950, 6" x 5", embossed bear.
Marked: Greetings Inc. $3.00 – 8.00.

Birthday, HD 1955, 5¼" x 4½",
embossed. Marked: The DA Line.
$3.00 – 6.00.

Birthday, c. 1943, 4¼" x 4¼", dog on rocking toy.
Marked: Hallmark. $3.00 – 6.00.

Birthday, 5" x 4". Marked: Rust Craft.
$3.00 – 8.00.

Holidays

Christmas

Santa, 5½" x 4¼", "Here Comes Santa," blue background. $3.00 – 6.00.

Santa, HD 1954, 5¾" x 4¾", Santa's hat folds over for 3-D effect. $3.00 – 8.00.

Santa, c. 1943, 4" x 4¼". Marked: Hallmark. $3.00 – 6.00.

Santa, HD 1948, 5" x 6", inspired by the immortal poem "Twas the Night Before Christmas," written by Clement Moore. Marked: Rynart. $3.00 – 6.00.

Santa, 4¾" x 4¾", feather attachment on beard. Marked: Whit. $3.00 – 6.00.

Santa, 4¾" x 4". Marked: Hallmark. $3.00 – 5.00.

Santa, 6¼" x 4", flocked suit. $4.00 – 10.00.

Santa, 6" x 5", flocked suit. Marked: A-Meri-Card. $4.00 – 10.00.

Santa, HD 1952, 5¾" x 4¾", attachment. $3.00 – 8.00.

Santa, HD 1948, 6" x 4½", flocked trim. $3.00 – 8.00.

Santa, 5¾" x 4", glitter. Marked: Hallmark. $4.00 – 8.00.

Santa, 5½" x 4½". $3.00 – 6.00.

Santa, 6" x 5", die-cut, pop-up, embossed. Marked: An Artistic Card. $4.00 – 10.00.

Santa, 6" x 4", feather attached to beard. Marked: Hallmark. $4.00 – 6.00.

Santa, 5½" x 4¼", unfolds to make an 8½" x 11" standing Santa. $4.00 – 8.00.

Santa, HD 1952, 5" x 4". Marked: Hallmark. $4.00 – 6.00.

Santa, HD 1952, 5¾" x 4¾", embossed Santa face and lettering. $4.00 – 8.00.

Santa, HD 1951, 4" x 4". Marked: Hallmark. $3.00 – 5.00.

Santa, 5½" x 4½". He's making a list and checking it twice. Marked: Stonybrook Line. $4.00 – 8.00.

Santa, 5" x 4¼", Santa plays bagpipes with Scottie dog at his feet. Marked: Wm. S Coutts Ltd. Canada. $4.00 – 8.00.

Santa, 4" x 4". Marked: Quality. $3.00 – 5.00.

Santa, 5¼" x 4¼", Santa checking list. $3.00 – 8.00.

Santa, HD 1942, 4½" x 3½", Santa Jack-in-the-box. Marked: McKenzie Greetings. $3.00 – 6.00.

Santa, 6" x 4", unique, unfolds three times to create a 16" x 11" message. $4.00 – 10.00.

Santa, 5½" x 4½", embossed. $3.00 – 6.00.

Santa, 4¼" x 3¾", inside is Santa with Scottie dog pulling Santa's beard. $3.00 – 6.00.

Santa, 5½" x 4½", embossed. $3.00 – 8.00.

Santa, 5¼" x 4¼".
$3.00 – 5.00.

Santa, 6" x 4¾". Marked: Grinnell. $3.00 – 5.00.

Santa, HD 1948, 5" x 4". Marked: R.R.H. $3.00 – 5.00.

Santa, 5" x 4". $3.00 – 5.00.

Santa, 5½" x 4½". Marked: American Greetings. $4.00 – 6.00.

Santa, HD 1942, 4½" x 3½". Marked: Crestwick. $2.00 – 4.00.

Santa, 5" x 4". $3.00 – 5.00.

Frosty the Snowman
Nelson/Rollins 1950

Frosty the Snowman was a jolly, happy soul,
With a corncob pipe and a button nose and two
Eyes made out of coal.
Frosty the snowman was a fairy tale they say...

Yes, Frosty is indeed a fairy tale, but a very popular one. His creators, Jack Nelson and Steve Rollins, wrote this catchy tune that was recorded by Gene Autry in 1950, following Autry's success with "Rudolph the Red Nosed Reindeer" the previous year. "Frosty the Snowman" turned out to be yet another hit, and the story it tells went down in history as another beloved Christmas legend. Snowmen have long been a popular subject for Christmas cards.

Most snowman cards after 1950 show a snowman sporting a top hat. This is perhaps because children know, from the song, that such hats will magically bring their snowmen to life just as one did for that jolly happy soul, Frosty.

Snowman, c. 1948, 9" x 7", glitter effect, fuzzy earmuff, easel back. Marked: Hallmark. $15.00 – 35.00.

Snowman, c. 1948, 5" x 3¼". Marked:
Hallmark. $3.00 – 5.00.

Snowman, HD 1953, 5¾" x 4¾", glitter. $3.00 –
6.00.

Snowman, HD 1953, 6" x 4", glitter. Marked:
Rust Craft. $3.00 – 6.00.

Snowman, c. 1952, 6" x 4", flocked. Marked:
Rust Craft. $3.00 – 6.00.

Snowman, 4¾" x 3¾". Marked: Hallmark. $2.00 – 4.00.

Snowman, 5" x 4". $2.00 – 4.00.

MERRY CHRISTMAS, GRANDPA

Snowman, 6½" x 3", glitter. Marked: Hallmark. $3.00 – 5.00.

Greetings

Snowman, 5¾" x 4¾", pop-up. $3.00 – 8.00.

Snowman, 6" x 4". $3.00 – 6.00.

Snowman, HD 1945, 5½" x 4½", package folded over for 3-D effect. $4.00 – 8.00.

Snowman, 7¼" x 3¼", glitter. Marked: Hallmark. $4.00 – 6.00.

Snowman, 5" x 4". $2.00 – 4.00.

Snowman, 5" x 4". Marked: Paramount. $2.00 – 4.00.

Snowman, 6" x 4", glitter. Marked: Rust Craft.
$4.00 – 8.00.

Snowman, 6" x 4", glitter. Marked: Paramount.
$4.00 – 8.00.

Snowman, HD 1945, 5" x 4". $3.00 – 5.00.

Snowman, HD 1955, 5½" x 4¼", flocked,
signed "JC Sax," nice graphics front, back,
and inside. Marked: Gibson. $4.00 –
8.00.

Snowman, 8" x 4", glitter. Marked:
Gibson. $4.00 – 6.00.

Rudolph, c. 1939 by Robert L. May, 6" x 5", boy cutout on front. $15.00 – 30.00.

Rudolph, the Red-Nosed Reindeer
Johnny Marks 1949

You know Dasher and Dancer and Prancer and Vixen,
Comet and Cupid and Donder and Blitzen,
But do you recall
The most famous reindeer of all?
Rudolph the Red-Nosed Reindeer
Had a very shiny nose,
And if you ever saw it,
You could even say it glows.
All of the other reindeer
Used to laugh and call him names,
They never let poor Rudolph
Join in any reindeer games.
Then one foggy Christmas Eve,
Santa came to say,
Rudolph with your nose so bright,
Won't you guide my sleigh tonight?
Then how the reindeer loved him
As they shouted out with glee,
"Rudolph the Red-Nosed Reindeer,
You'll go down in history!"

Rudolph began appearing on Christmas cards in 1940, and he remains a popular theme to this day. Although reindeer appeared on cards long before Rudolph, it was in 1939 that Rudolph the Red-Nosed Reindeer was born. That year Montgomery Ward department stores assigned employee Robert L. May the task of making a Christmas story coloring book for a promotional giveaway. May created the story of Rudolph, Denver Gillen from Montgomery Ward's art department sketched the delightful little deer, and a classic was born. Montgomery Ward gave away 2.4 million copies of the booklet in 1939, and by 1946, 6 million copies had been given away.

In 1947 *Rudolph the Red-Nosed Reindeer* was printed commercially, and a year later became a nine-minute cartoon shown in theaters. But the most famous promotion of all came in 1949, when Robert May's brother-in-law, Johnny Marks, wrote the lyrics and melody for the song. Recorded in 1949 by Gene Autry, it was an instant hit, selling over 2 million records.

Greeting cards featuring this classic Christmas character are very collectible and delight children of all ages. No Christmas card collection would be complete without Rudolph and his friends.

Rudolph, c. 1939 by Robert L. May, 6" x 5", Rudolph cutout on front. $15.00 – 30.00.

Rudolph, c. 1939 by Robert L. May, 6" x 5", die-cut stop-light opens to become Rudolph's nose. $15.00 – 30.00.

Rudolph, c. 1939 Robert L. May, 6" x 5", pop-up inside of Santa riding Rudolph. $15.00 – 30.00.

Rudolph, c. 1939 by Robert L. May, 6" x 5", pop-up inside of Rudolph kicking up his heels. $15.00 – 30.00.

Reindeer, 6½" x 4½", glitter. Marked:
Paramount. $4.00 – 8.00.

Reindeer, c. 1946, 5¾" x 4", glitter.
Marked: Hallmark. $4.00 – 6.00.

Reindeer, 6" x 4". Marked: Rust Craft.
$4.00 – 6.00.

Reindeer, HD 1946, 5½" x 4½". Marked: American
Greetings. $4.00 – 8.00.

Reindeer, HD 1953, 5¾" x 4¼". $2.00 – 4.00.

Reindeer, c. 1947, 4¾" x 3½". Marked: Hallmark. $4.00 – 6.00.

Reindeer, 6" x 5", attachment. $4.00 – 6.00.

Reindeer, HD 1946, 5" x 3½". Marked: The Wishing Well. $4.00 – 6.00.

Reindeer, 5½" x 4¾", embossed. Marked: Hallmark. $3.00 – 6.00.

Reindeer, IID 1958, 6" x 4½", embossed. $4.00 – 8.00.

Reindeer, 6" x 5", glitter. Marked: Norcross. $3.00 – 5.00.

Reindeer, 6" x 4". $3.00 – 6.00.

Girl, c. 1949, 7½" x 5", honeycomb tissue skirt on stiff card. Marked: Barker. $15.00 – 30.00.

Girl, PM 1930, 4¾" x 3½", one-sided. $4.00 – 8.00.

Girl, 5¾" x 4¾". Marked: American Greetings. $4.00 –
8.00.

Child, 1930s, 4" x 2¾", opens, heavy card stock. $4.00 – 8.00.

Boy, c. 1948, 4¾" x 4½", flocked. Marked: Hallmark.
$4.00 – 8.00.

Girl, c. 1948, 6" x 4", fuzzy trim on end of hat. Marked: Hallmark. $4.00 – 8.00.

Girl with Kittens, HD 1954, 6" x 4", flocked. Marked: Hallmark. $4.00 – 8.00.

Girl with Presents, HD 1954, 6" x 4", synthetic hair attached. Marked: Paramount. $4.00 – 10.00.

Children, c. 1942, 5" x 4¾", attached fringe trim on horse's mane. Marked: Hallmark. $4.00 – 10.00.

Children, 1930s, 4" x 4¾", one-sided. $4.00 – 8.00.

Girl beside Fire, 5" x 4½". Marked: Quality. $4.00 – 8.00.

Boy with Presents, 5" x 5", flocked. Marked: American Greetings. $4.00 – 8.00.

Boy with Puppy, 6" x 3½". $4.00 – 8.00.

Stockings, 4" x 4½", one-sided, embossed. $4.00 – 6.00.

Girl, HD 1951, 4½" x 4". Marked: Hallmark. $4.00 – 6.00.

Girl and Tree, HD 1946, 6" x 5", inside are decorations to cut out and put on tree. Marked: G.B. $4.00 – 6.00.

Boy with Shovel, 4½" x 4". Marked: Stanley. $4.00 – 6.00.

Girl at Mailbox, HD 1948, 5" x 4". Marked: Volland. $4.00 – 6.00.

Boy with Candy Cane, c. 1946, 5¾" x 4", glitter. Marked: Hallmark. $4.00 – 8.00.

Girl and Stocking, c. 1947, 6¾" x 4", flocked. Marked: Hallmark. $4.00 – 8.00.

Puppy in Stocking, c. 1944, 6¼" x 3½", flocked. Marked: Hallmark. $4.00 – 6.00.

Children, 4¼" x 4¼". $3.00 – 5.00.

Boy and Dog, HD 1952, 5¼" x 4½", flocked. Marked: Norcross. $4.00 – 6.00.

Girl, HD 1949, 6" x 4". Marked: The Wishing Well. $4.00 – 8.00.

Children, HD 1951, 5½" x 4½", folds to 3-D stand-up, signed "Eva Harta." $3.00 – 6.00.

Girl, 1944, 3" x 5". Marked: A Hallmark Card. $5.00 – 10.00.

Let it Snow...

Fun in the snow is a very popular subject for children's Christmas cards. As you look through this section, you can almost hear the giggles and the squeals of excitement as the children play in the snow.

Pup on Skates, 5¾" x 4¼", flocked. $3.00 – 6.00.

Boy on Sled, 6" x 4¾", folds out for 3-D effect. Marked: Norcross. $3.00 – 8.00.

Boy on Sled, 6¼" x 4½", embossed. Marked: Hallmark. $3.00 – 6.00.

Boy with Snowballs, 6" x 4", flocked. Marked: Norcross. $3.00 – 6.00.

Boy and Dog, 7" x 3½", flocked.
Marked: Hallmark "Slim Jims."
$4.00 – 6.00.

Child on Skates, 6½" x 4½", flocked, tabs fold
for standing card up. Marked: A-Meri-Card.
$3.00 – 8.00.

Boy on Skates, 7" x 3¼", flocked.
Marked: Hallmark. $3.00 – 6.00.

Child on Block of Ice, 6" x 5", embossed. Marked: A-
Meri-Card. $3.00 – 8.00.

Easter

Bunnies, HD 1949, 8½" x 6¾", cut-out wheels turn open to stand card up. Marked: Norcross. $10.00 – 40.00.

Boy and Bunny, c. 1948, 8¾" x 7", easel backed, flocked. Marked: Hallmark. $10.00 – 20.00.

Bunnies, c. 1949, 4¾" x 4½", flocked. Marked: Hallmark. $4.00 – 8.00.

Lambs, c. 1945, 4¼" x 4". Marked: Hallmark. $4.00 – 6.00.

Child and Bunnies, c. 1943, 6" x 4", flocked. Marked: Hallmark. $4.00 – 8.00.

Bunnies, 6" x 4½", baby bunny comes out to open its own greeting. Marked: Norcross "A Double Wish Card." $5.00 – 10.00.

Bunny, c. 1949, 5" x 4", flocked. Marked: Hallmark. $4.00 – 8.00.

Boy and Bunnies, 6" x 4", glitter. Marked: Rust Craft. $3.00 – 6.00.

Boy and Bunnies, 5" x 4", flocked. Marked: Hallmark. $4.00 – 8.00.

Child Dressed as Bunny, HD 1950, 5½" x 4". Marked: Gibson. $4.00 – 6.00.

141

Girl and Lamb, c. 1948, 4¾" x 4½", flocked. Marked: Hallmark. $4.00 – 8.00.

Ducklings, c. 1949, 4¾" x 4½", flocked. Marked: Hallmark. $4.00 – 6.00.

Bunny, HD 1951, 5" x 4½", flocked. Marked: Hallmark. $4.00 – 8.00.

Angels, 5¼" x 4½", tri-fold opens to show six little girl angels 13" long. Marked: Norcross. $4.00 – 8.00.

Chicks, 6" x 4", flocked. Marked: Rust Craft. $4.00 – 6.00.

Boy and Bunny, HD 1952, 5¾" x 4". Marked: Hallmark. $4.00 – 6.00.

Boy and Barrel, c. 1945, 5¾" x 4", cloth hanky attachment on hip pocket. Marked: Hallmark. $4.00 – 8.00.

Girl with Bunny, 5" x 3¾". Marked: Hallmark. $3.00 – 6.00.

Girl with Flowers, HD 1949, 6" x 4¼". Marked: Gibson. $4.00 – 6.00.

Girl and Eggs, HD 1957, 6¾" x 3¾", glitter. Marked: Hallmark. $4.00 – 8.00.

Boy and Bunny, 6" x 4", glitter. Marked: Rust Craft. $3.00 – 6.00.

Boy and Bunnies, 5½" x 4½", tri-fold, opens to picture 12¼" tall. Marked: made in Canada. $3.00 – 6.00.

143

Bunny, c. 1949, 4½" x 3½". Marked: Hallmark. $3.00 – 6.00.

Chicks, c. 1947, 5¼" x 4", lace veil attachment on black duck's hat. Marked: Peeper and Peep, Charles Christian Culp. $4.00 – 8.00.

Boy and Animals, c. 1948, 6" x 4", boy has synthetic hair. Marked: Tommy and His Turtle, Hallmark. $4.00 – 8.00.

Bunny in Train, 4¼" x 3¼", tri-fold, opens to 12". Marked: Norcross. $4.00 – 8.00.

Boy and Duck, 5½" x 4½". Marked: Norcross. $3.00 – 6.00.

Valentine's Day

Children, HD 1948, 8" x 9½", girl moves and picture on TV changes, tabs to stand card up. $15.00 – 30.00.

Children, 5½" x 4½". Marked: Carrington Co. $4.00 – 8.00.

Queen of Hearts, HD 1955, 5½" x 3¾". Marked: Hallmark. $4.00 – 8.00.

Boy and Gift, HD 1954, 5" x 4". Marked: Paramount. $4.00 – 6.00.

Bunny, HD 1953, 4¼" x 3½". Marked: Hallmark. $3.00 – 6.00.

Boy in Car, HD 1951, 4¾" x 3¾". Marked: Gibson. $3.00 – 6.00.

Girl with Heart, HD 1953, 5" x 3¼".
Marked: Hallmark. $3.00 – 6.00.

Girl with Heart, c. 1948, 5¾" x 4½", yarn bow
attached on hair. Marked: Doodles, Hallmark.
$4.00 – 6.00.

Boy and Girl, HD 1945, 5" x 4". Marked:
Carrington Co. $3.00 – 6.00.

Girl with Heart, c. 1943, 6" x 4",
feather attachment. Marked: Hallmark. $4.00 – 10.00.

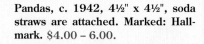

Pandas, c. 1942, 4½" x 4½", soda
straws are attached. Marked: Hallmark. $4.00 – 6.00.

Boy at Box, HD 1950, 6" x 4". Marked:
Hallmark. $4.00 – 6.00.

Boy Whistling, 5" x 4¼", tri-fold, opens out to 11½". $3.00 – 6.00.

Bear, c. 1945, 6" x 4", flocked. Marked: Hallmark. $4.00 – 8.00.

Children, 4½" x 3½". Marked: Volland. $3.00 – 6.00.

Children's Band, 8½" x 4¾", drum has honeycomb tissue, fold-out tabs for standing card up. $8.00 – 20.00.

Girl and Cats, HD 1955, 4¾" x 3¾". Marked: Gibson. $4.00 – 8.00.

Children, 5" x 3¼", one-sided, mechanical. $5.00 – 15.00.

Boy with Hat, 6" x 4½", one-sided, feather attachment. $5.00 – 10.00.

Children Reading, 4½" x 3½". Marked: Volland. $4.00 – 6.00.

Girl with Hearts, HD 1953, 7¾" x 6¼", mechanical top half moves side-to-side, legs also move separately. Marked: Hallmark. $5.00 – 30.00.

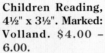

Children, 4¾" x 3¾", one-sided, foldback tabs, unsigned but attributed to Grace Drayton. $5.00 – 35.00.

Boy and Girl, 4" x 3¾", one-sided tabs to stand up, unsigned but attributed to Grace Drayton, creator of the Campbell's Kids. $5.00 – 35.00.

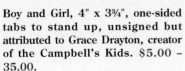

Romeo and Juliet, 3½" x 2¾". Marked: Carring-ton. $5.00 – 8.00.

Boy and Girl, 4" x 3¼". Marked: A-Meri-Card. $2.00 – 5.00.

Boy Holding Flowers, 9¾" x 6"; arm, flowers, and right leg move; stand-up. Marked: Whitney. $10.00 – 20.00.

Miscellaneous

Buttons

Little Girl, HD 1945, 5¾" x 4¾", button attachment. Marked: Forget-Me-Not. $5.00 – 8.00.

A New Father, c. 1945, 5¼" x 4¼", button attachment. Marked: Hallmark. $5.00 – 8.00.

Birthday, c. 1941, 4¾" x 4", button attachment. Marked: Hallmark. $5.00 – 8.00.

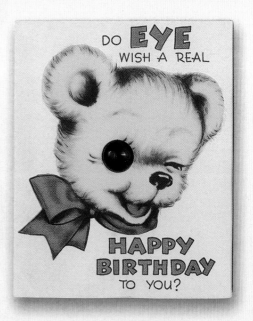

Bear, 4¾" x 4", button attachment. $5.00 – 8.00.

Shapes

Bear, c. 1946, 5¾" x 3¾", button attachment. Marked: Hallmark. $5.00 – 8.00.

House, 5¼" x 4¼", glitter. Marked: Norcross. $4.00 – 8.00.

Oven, 5¼" x 4¼". Marked: Norcross. $4.00 – 8.00.

Cupboard, 5½" x 4½". Marked: Norcross. $4.00 – 8.00.

Cash Register, 5¼" x 4½". Marked: Norcross. $4.00 – 8.00.

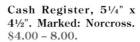

Soda Carton, 5¼" x 4½". Marked: Norcross. $4.00 – 8.00.

151

Mug, 6¾" x 4". Marked: Klever Kards by Renner Davis. $4.00 – 8.00.

Playhouse, HD 1954, 5¼" x 4¼". Marked: American Greetings. $4.00 – 8.00.

Jack-in-the-Box, c. 1943, 5¾" x 4½", felt gloves attached. Marked: Hallmark. $4.00 – 8.00.

Record Player. Marked: Norcross. $4.00 – 8.00.

Patriotic

GIs and Nurse, c. 1942, 5½" x 5", cloth flag attached. Marked: Hallmark. $5.00 – 10.00.

Colonial Couple, c. 1942, 5¾" x 4", flocked. Marked: Hallmark. $5.00 – 10.00.

Plane, c. 1942, 4" x 4¼". Marked: Hallmark. $5.00 – 10.00.

Jeep, HD 1944, 4½" x 4½". $5.00 – 10.00.

Tank. $5.00 – 10.00.

Drummer Boy, 5" x 3". Marked: Paramount. $4.00 – 6.00.

Boy Pretending, 5½" x 3½". Marked: Paramount. $4.00 – 6.00.

Colonial Couple, c. 1941, 5" x 4". Marked: Hallmark. $4.00 – 6.00.

Records

Inside of or on the front of each card is an actual 33⅓ rpm record.

Birthday, c. 1964, 6" x 6", Alvin and the Chipmunks. Marked: Buzza Cardozo. $5.00 – 12.00.

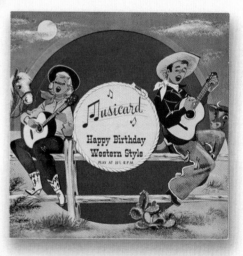

A Musicard, c. 1958, 7" x 7". Marked: Fairfield. $5.00 – 25.00.

A Musicard c. 1958, 7" x 7". Marked: Fairfield. $5.00 – 25.00.

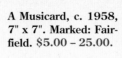

A Musicard, c. 1958, 7" x 7". Marked: Fairfield. $5.00 – 25.00.

School Days

A Musicard, c. 1958, 7" x 7". Marked: Fairfield. $5.00 – 25.00.

Birthday, 5¾" x 4¾", feather attachment. Marked: Quality. $4.00 – 8.00.

Valentine, 4¾" x 3¾". Marked: American Greetings. $3.00 – 6.00.

Birthday, 5½" x 4½". Marked: American Greetings. $4.00 – 6.00.

Birthday, 5¼" x 4¼". $4.00 – 8.00.

Birthday, 1976, 6¼" x 4". Marked: Buzza Cardozo. $2.00 – 4.00.

Birthday. $4.00 – 8.00.

Birthday, 6¾" x 4½". Marked: Wishing Well Greetings. $4.00 – 6.00.

Birthday, HD 1955, 5½" x 4½". Marked: Norcross. $4.00 – 6.00.

Televisions

Santa, 6" x 4½", television movie, Santa inside moves as he is playing the piano. $4.00 – 6.00.

Family Gathered, 5½" x 4½", embossed. $4.00 – 6.00.

Daddy Birthday, HD 1954, 5½" x 4½", die-cut, pop-up. Marked: Norcross. $4.00 – 6.00.

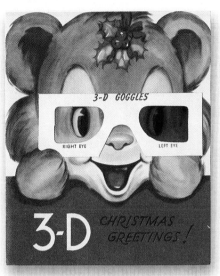

Puppies, HD 1955, 6" x 4¾". Marked: Forget-me-not. $4.00 – 6.00.

Bear, 6" x 5", attached 3-D goggles can be used to view the picture inside card. $4.00 – 8.00.

Bunny, HD 1951, 5¼" x 5¼", toy card, chain attachment is part of face in picture (tap it around and make a nose and mouth). Marked: Hallmark. $4.00 – 8.00.

Children and Cake, c. 1948. 4½" x 5", talking card, says "Happy Birthday!" when you run your thumbnail over the cord. Marked: A Nova Laugh. $5.00 – 10.00.

Girl, c. 1945, 5¾" x 4½", two front teeth attached. Marked: a Barker Card. $4.00 – 8.00.

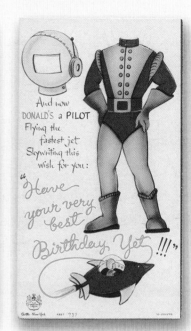

Boy and Oar, 7" x 4", Donald, boy paper doll says "Happy Birthday to a Fine Boy," has five punch-out outfits. Marked: Gato. $10.00 – 55.00.

Boy with Letters, HD 1948, 5¾" x 5", surprise card is tiny card in a tiny envelope that is inside a bit larger one that is inside an even larger one. Marked: Forget-Me-Not. $4.00 – 10.00.

Postal Bear, c. 1941, 6¾" x 5½", eight-envelope surprise card, each envelope smaller than last, part of message on each envelope. Marked: Hallmark. $4.00 – 10.00.

Pets

What child doesn't giggle and smile at the sight of a frisky little puppy? Card makers have been delighting children with images of puppies and dogs all through the years. The 1930s and 1940s brought an abundance of Scottish terrier images. These were made popular by president Franklin D. Roosevelt's constant Scottie companion, Fala.

Also from this same period, cards featuring wire-haired terriers were popular, perhaps due to the hit series of *The Thin Man* movies (1934 – 1947) staring William Powell and Myrna Loy with their delightful wire-haired terrier dog, Asta.

In 1950, Greetings Inc. created a set of die-cut figural dog cards of many different breeds. They were printed on both front and back. The greeting tag was removable, and the card could be stood up for display. The same card can be found with a variety of greetings, from "Happy Birthday" to "Get Well." The first cards carried a small paragraph inside describing the characteristics of that breed, plus the actual greeting message. Later printings of these cards did not include the breed description. The copyright date is 1950, but cards are found hand-dated well into the 1950s.

A similar set was marked "Bow Wow cards by Sterling." These cards, though nice, do not have the deep embossing and vivid colors used by Greetings Inc.

Dog cards can be found in every size, shape, and description imaginable, from ones that look like various breeds to comic dogs, dogs dressed as people doing human jobs, dogs playing with children's toys, or dogs just being perky little puppies. Dog cards are fun to collect and readily available, and most dog cards are reasonably priced.

Dogs and Puppies

Greetings Inc. Series, c. 1950, 6" x 5", embossed, removable greeting tag, beagle and tag are both printed front and back. Marked: Greetings Inc. $5.00 – 15.00.

Boxer, c. 1950, 6" x 5", removable greeting tag. Marked: Greetings Inc. $5.00 – 15.00.

Cocker, c. 1950, 6" x 5", die-cut, embossed, removable greeting tag. Marked: Greetings Inc. $5.00 – 15.00.

Collie, c. 1950, 6" x 5", embossed, removable greeting tag. Marked: Greetings Inc. $5.00 – 15.00.

Fox Terrier, c. 1950, 6" x 5", embossed, removable greeting tag. Marked: Greetings Inc. $5.00 – 15.00.

Pomeranian, c. 1950, 6" x 5",
embossed, removable greeting tag.
Marked: Greetings Inc. $5.00 –
15.00.

Pekingese, c. 1950, 6" x 5",
embossed, removable greeting tag.
Marked: Greetings Inc. $5.00 –
15.00.

Springer Spaniel, c. 1950, 6" x 5",
embossed, removable greeting tag.
Marked: Greetings Inc. $5.00 –
15.00.

Scottie, c. 1950, 6" x 5", embossed,
removable greeting tag. Marked:
Greetings Inc. $10.00 – 25.00.

Bow Wows by Sterling, HD 1950,
6" x 5", embossed, removable
greeting tag, fox terrier. Marked:
Sterling. $4.00 – 8.00.

Bow Wows by Sterling, 6" x 5",
embossed, removable greeting tag,
Dalmatian. Marked: Sterling.
$4.00 – 8.00.

Bow Wows by Sterling, 6" x 5",
embossed, removable greeting tag,
Boston bull. Marked: Sterling.
$4.00 – 8.00.

Bow Wows by Sterling, 6" x 5",
embossed, removable greeting tag,
collie. Marked: Sterling. $4.00 –
8.00.

Pup with Flowers, 6½" x 5½", inside
is a Jack-in-the-box with clown
attached with spring. Marked: Gibson.
$4.00 – 8.00.

161

Pups in Doghouse, 6" x 5", embossed.
Marked: Fairfield. $4.00 – 8.00.

With Bow, c. 1947, 5¾" x 4".
Marked: Hallmark. $4.00 – 8.00.

Flower in Mouth, HD 1948, 5¾"
x 4¾". Marked: The DA Line.
$4.00 – 8.00.

In Bath, c. 1947, 5" x 4", glitter.
Marked: Hallmark. $4.00 – 8.00.

With Holly, 7" x 5¾", attached
bead eyes. Marked: Norcross.
$4.00 – 10.00.

On Swing, 6" x 5¾", can be stood
up and will rock back and forth.
Marked: A Rock-It card, H.A. Co.
$4.00 – 6.00.

Sipping Soda, 6" x 4¼". Marked:
A Sunshine Card. $4.00 – 6.00.

Pulling Wagon, 5½" x 4¼",
flocked. Marked: Gibson.
$4.00 – 6.00.

On Ferris Wheel, 4½" x 4¾".
Marked: Gibson. $3.00 – 5.00.

On Wheels, c. 1944, 4¾" x 4¾", flocked.
Marked: Hallmark. $4.00 – 8.00.

With Sailboat, 5½" x 4¼", flocked.
Marked: Gibson. $4.00 – 6.00.

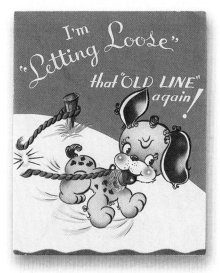

Tugging Rope, comic, 5¾" x 4¾",
embossed, attached collar. Marked:
Quality. $4.00 – 8.00.

Scratching Ear, comic, 5¾" x 4¾".
Marked: American Greetings. $4.00 –
6.00.

With Bandage, comic, 5¾" x 4¾",
attached, die-cut leg. Marked: Renner
Davis "Klever Kards". $4.00 – 8.00.

With Doghouse, comic, 5" x 4¾". $4.00 –
6.00.

Bundled Up, comic, 5¾" x 4¾", six-page
get well message. Marked: Forget-Me-
Not. $4.00 – 6.00.

With Heart, 8¾" x 7", feather
attached, easel back. Marked: Hallmark. $5.00 – 10.00.

163

Cats and Kittens

With Basket, c. 1945, 6" x 4",
ribbon attachment. Marked: Hallmark. $4.00 – 8.00.

On Stage, 5¾" x 4¼",
novel fold, opens to 17"
long. $4.00 – 8.00.

With Flowerpot, 4" x 4½", flocked.
Marked: Hallmark. $4.00 – 8.00.

In Cookie Jar, 5¾" x 4¾". Marked:
American Greetings. $4.00 – 8.00.

In Apron, 5½" x 4½". Marked: Norcross. $4.00 – 6.00.

In Cookie Jar, c. 1944, 4½" x 4".
Marked: Hallmark. $4.00 – 6.00.

Fishing, HD 1952, 5½" x 4½". Marked:
Forget-Me-Not. $4.00 – 6.00.

Looking in Mirror, 6" x 5". Marked:
Harry Doehla Company. $4.00 – 8.00.

In Basket, 4½" x 4¾". Marked: Hall-mark. $4.00 – 6.00.

With Yarn, 5½" x 3¾", flocked. Marked: Hallmark. $4.00 – 6.00.

Hearing a Bedtime Story, 5¾" x 4¾", embossed. Marked: S.co. $4.00 – 6.00.

With Holly, 5¾" x 4¾", embossed. Marked: An Artistic Card. $4.00 – 6.00.

Playing with Yarn, 5¾" x 4½", embossed. Marked: Wishing Well Greetings. $4.00 – 6.00.

On Roller Coaster, 6" x 4", tri-fold. Marked: Rust Craft. $4.00 – 6.00.

Wearing Bow, c. 1950, 5¾" x 5", embossed, printed on front and back, removable greeting tag (like the dog series). Marked: Greetings Inc. $4.00 – 8.00.

Wearing Bow, c. 1940, 5¼" x 3¼". Marked: Hallmark. $4.00 – 6.00.

165

On Slide, 6½" x 4¼", glitter.
$4.00 – 8.00.

Wearing Sign, c. 1936, 4" x 3",
party invitation. Marked: Rust Craft.
$2.00 – 5.00.

Wearing Ribbon, 5¾" x 4¾", tri-fold.
$4.00 – 6.00.

Kitten and Pup Reading Book, c. 1939, 5" x
4". Marked: Rust Craft. $4.00 – 6.00.

Kitten and Pup at Well, c. 1950, 6" x 4".
Marked: Rust Craft. $4.00 – 6.00.

Holding Card, HD 1943, 5½" x
3¼". Marked: Gibson. $4.00 –
6.00.

Signed by Artist

Angela

    The unique and whimsical style of the artist Angela is unmistakable. Her work featuring children, angels, fairies, and animals has delighted many for decades.

    She was a prolific artist, producing hundreds of greeting card designs for the Fravessi LaMont company during the 1940s. Information about this artist remains elusive, however. She signed all her work with just one name, "Angela"; the mystery of the artist and the charm of her style make her work highly collectible.

5" x 5". Marked: Frevessi LaMont. $5.00 – 10.00.

6" x 4". Marked: Frevessi LaMont. $5.00 – 10.00.

5" x 4". Marked: Frevessi LaMont. $5.00 – 10.00.

5" x 5", Marked: Frevessi LaMont. $5.00 – 10.00.

Open view of preceding card.

Jt might rain cats and dogs
Or even little fishes
But since it is your birthday
Jt's raining Best of Wishes

Happy Birthday

4" x 4". Marked: Frevessi LaMont. $5.00 – 10.00.

6½" x 4½". Marked: Frevessi LaMont. $5.00 – 10.00.

5" x 4". Marked: Frevessi LaMont. $5.00 – 10.00.

5" x 4". Marked: Frevessi LaMont. $5.00 – 10.00.

5" x 4". **Marked: Frevessi LaMont.** $5.00 – 10.00.

5" x 5". **Marked: Frevessi LaMont.** $5.00 – 10.00.

5" x 4". **Marked: Frevessi LaMont.** $5.00 – 10.00.

4" x 5". **Marked: Frevessi LaMont.** $5.00 – 10.00.

5" x 4". Marked: Frevessi LaMont. $5.00 – 10.00.

3¼" x 4¼". Marked: Frevessi LaMont. $5.00 – 10.00.

5" x 4". Marked: Frevessi LaMont. $5.00 – 10.00.

6¼" x 4½". Marked: Frevessi LaMont. $5.00 – 10.00.

Mabel Lucie Attwell
1879 – 1964

British artist Mable Lucie Attwell began her career at the age of 16 and went on to become one of the most popular illustrators in Great Britain. Her illustrations can be found in numerous children's books, on postcards, and on greeting cards. Her children's images adorn children's china, fabric, and much more. Sets of Attwell china were used in the royal nursery by Princesses Margaret and Elizabeth of Great Britain, and later by Queen Elizabeth's children.

By 1911, Valentine and Sons of Dundee began to print her illustrations on postcards and greeting cards, and it still reproduces much of her work to this day.

Copyright 1991, 7¾" x 5½". Marked: Made in U.K. by Valentines. $5.00 – 10.00.

Copyright 1991, 7¾" x 5½". Marked: Made in U.K. by Valentines. $5.00 – 10.00.

Copyright 1991, 7¾" x 5½". Marked: Made in U.K. by Valentines. $5.00 – 10.00.

Copyright 1991, 7¾" x 5½". Marked: Made in U.K. by Valentines. $5.00 – 10.00.

171

Copyright 1991, 7¾" x 5½". Marked: Made in U.K. by Valentines. $5.00 – 10.00.

Copyright 1991, 7¾" x 5½". Marked: Made in U.K. by Valentines. $5.00 – 10.00.

Copyright 1991, 7¾" x 5½". Marked: Made in U.K. by Valentines. $5.00 – 10.00.

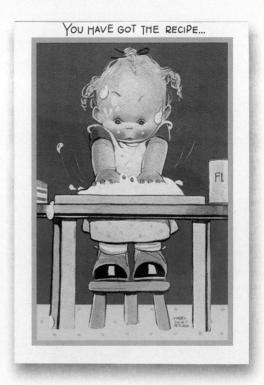

Copyright 1991, 7¾" x 5½". Marked: Made in U.K. by Valentines. $5.00 – 10.00.

Copyright 1991, 7¾" x 5½". Marked: Made in U.K. by Valentines. $5.00 – 10.00.

Copyright 1991, 7¾" x 5½". Marked: Made in U.K. by Valentines. $5.00 – 10.00.

Copyright 1991, 7¾" x 5½". Marked: Made in U.K. by Valentines. $5.00 – 10.00.

Copyright 1991, 7¾" x 5½". Marked: Made in U.K. by Valentines. $5.00 – 10.00.

Charlot Byj
1920 – 1983

The whimsical children created by this artist are found on greeting cards from the 1940s and 1950s, and many are being reproduced even now. The most famous of her characters are the members of the O'Hair family. Shabby O'Hair, a mischievous little redheaded boy, seems to always be up to something; his little sister, Raggy Muffin O'Hair, is adorable; and M'lady O'Hair is the plumb little mama character.

These little redheaded characters caught the attention of Franz Goebel of the Goebel company, maker of Hummel figurines. He invited Charlot to visit Goebel in Germany and, as they say, "the rest is history." Goebel began producing the Charlot Byj redheads as figurines in 1957 and continued the line until 1988. More than 100 different designs were produced.

The O'Hair cards are favorites of many collectors, while others can't resist Byj's adorable toddler and baby cards. She designed not only children, but also Christmas cards and animals.

Look closely for her signature, as it is often difficult to see within a design.

Valentine, c. 1946, 5" x 5", little redhead reading Romeo and Juliet. Marked: Ars sacra Hubert Dubler Inc. $15.00 – 45.00.

Shabby O'Hair card, c. 1944, 4½" x 4¼". Marked: Ars sacra Hubert Dubler Inc. $5.00 – 10.00.

Shabby O'Hair, birthday, c. 1944, 4½" x 4¼". Marked: Crestwick. $5.00 – 10.00.

Shabby O'Hair card, c. 1944, 4½" x 4¼". Marked: Ars sacra Hubert Dubler Inc. $5.00 – 10.00.

An O'Hair original, this is Shabby's sister, Raggy Muffin O'Hair, 5½" x 4¼". Marked: Crestwick-Hummelwerk. $5.00 – 10.00.

5½" x 4¼". Marked: Crestwick. $5.00 – 10.00.

An O'Hair original, Raggy Muffin O'Hair; 5½"
x 4¼". Marked: Crestwick. $5.00 – 10.00.

This is Shabby's mom, M'lady O'Hair; c. 1945,
5" x 4". Marked: Ars sacra Hubert Dubler Inc.
$5.00 – 10.00.

This is Z Zithy Birdbrain; 5" x 4". Blank note
cards came as a boxed set with eight different
Zithy designs (seven shown). $5.00 – 10.00.

Z Zithy Birdbrain, 5" x 4", blank note card.
$5.00 – 10.00.

Z Zithy Birdbrain, 5" x 4", blank note card.
$5.00 – 10.00.

Z Zithy Birdbrain, 5" x 4", blank note card.
$5.00 – 10.00.

Z Zithy Birdbrain, 5" x 4", blank note card.
$5.00 – 10.00.

Z Zithy Birdbrain, 5" x 4", blank note card.
$5.00 – 10.00.

Z Zithy Birdbrain, 5" x 4", blank note card.
$5.00 – 10.00.

Sweet 'n Saucy All Occasion box for 20 note cards,
5¼" x 5¼". $5.00 – 10.00.

Sweet 'n Saucy, 4¾" x 4¾". $5.00 – 10.00.

Sweet 'n Saucy, 4¾" x 4¾". $5.00 – 10.00.

Sweet 'n Saucy, 4¾" x 4¾". Marked: a Doehla fine arts Card. $5.00 – 10.00.

Sweet 'n Saucy, 4¾" x 4¾". $5.00 – 10.00.

Sweet 'n Saucy, 4¾" x 4¾". $5.00 – 10.00.

Sweet 'n Saucy, 4¾" x 4¾". $5.00 – 10.00.

Sweet 'n Saucy, 4¾" x 4¾". $5.00 – 10.00.

Sweet 'n Saucy, 4¾" x 4¾". $5.00 – 10.00.

Sweet 'n Saucy, 4¾" x 4¾". $5.00 – 10.00.

Sweet 'n Saucy, 4¾" x 4¾". $5.00 – 10.00.

Sweet 'n Saucy, 4¾" x 4¾". $5.00 – 10.00.

Sweet 'n Saucy, 4¾" x 4¾". Marked: a Doehla fine arts
Card. $5.00 – 10.00.

Sweet 'n Saucy, 4¾" x 4¾". Marked: a Doehla fine arts
Card. $5.00 – 10.00.

Sweet 'n Saucy, 4¾" x 4¾". $5.00 – 10.00.

Sweet 'n Saucy, 4¾" x 4¾". Marked: a Doehla fine arts Card. $5.00 – 10.00.

Box for Whipper Snapper Cards, 5½" x 5½". Each card in this set has the Top Honors baby logo on back. $5.00 – 10.00.

Whipper Snappers, 5" x 5". $5.00 – 10.00.

Whipper Snappers, 5" x 5". $5.00 – 10.00.

Whipper Snappers, 5" x 5". $5.00 – 10.00.

Whipper Snappers, 5" x 5". $5.00 – 10.00.

Whipper Snappers, 5" x 5". $5.00 – 10.00.

Whipper Snappers, 5" x 5". $5.00 – 10.00.

Whipper Snappers, 5" x 5". $5.00 – 10.00.

Whipper Snappers, 5" x 5". $5.00 – 10.00.

Whipper Snappers, 5" x 5". $5.00 – 10.00.

Whipper Snappers, 5" x 5". $5.00 – 10.00.

Whipper Snappers, 5" x 5". $5.00 – 10.00.

Whipper Snappers, 5" x 5. $5.00 – 10.00.

Whipper Snappers, 5" x 5". $5.00 – 10.00.

Whipper Snappers, 5" x 5". $5.00 – 10.00.

184

Marjorie Cooper

Illustrations by Marjorie Cooper appeared on cards from Rust Craft Publishers throughout the 1940s and into the 1950s. Marjorie was a member of the Rust Craft Artist Guild. Her work primarily featured children and animals, but can be found in many different styles. Her work was signed "Marjorie Cooper," "M. Cooper," or just "MC." An unusual signature is shown on one of the cards pictured here; it was printed in reverse. Look for individual cards as well as boxed sets, all occasion cards, blank notes, and Christmas cards.

Copyright 1945, 5¾" x 5¼", inside has larger copy of picture on front. Marked: Rust Craft. $4.00 – 6.00.

Copyright 1945, 4½" x 4¼". Marked: Rust Craft. $3.00 – 5.00.

Copyright 1945, 4½" x 4¼". Marked: Rust Craft. $3.00 – 5.00.

Copyright 1946, 4½" x 4¼". Marked: Rust Craft. $3.00 – 5.00.

Copyright 1946, 5" x 4". Marked: Rust Craft.
$3.00 – 5.00.

Copyright 1947, 6" x 4", printed front and
back. Marked: Rust Craft. $4.00 – 6.00.

5½" x 3½". Marked: Rust Craft. $3.00 –
5.00.

Copyright 1947, 6" x 4", printed on front
and back. Marked: Rust Craft. $4.00 –
6.00.

Copyright 1949, 6" x 4", tri-fold, opens to 12" picture. Marked: Rust Craft. $4.00 – 6.00.

Copyright 1949, 5¼" x 5½". Marked: Rust Craft. $3.00 – 5.00.

Copyright 1949, 5" x 4". Marked: Rust Craft. $3.00 – 5.00.

Copyright 1946, 5" x 4¾". Marked: Rust Craft. $3.00 – 5.00.

Copyright 1946, 5" x 4¾". Marked: Rust Craft. $3.00 –
5.00.

Copyright 1947, 5" x 4¾". Marked: Rust Craft. $3.00 –
5.00.

5" x 4¾". Marked: Rust Craft. $3.00 – 5.00.

Copyright 1947, 5" x 4¾", unique signature printed in
reverse. Marked: Rust Craft. $4.00 – 8.00.

Copyright 1948, 5" x 4¾". Marked: Rust Craft. $4.00 –
8.00.

Copyright 1951, 4½" x 4¼". Marked: Rust Craft.
$4.00 – 6.00.

5¼" x 4½". Marked: Rust Craft. $4.00 – 6.00.

5½" x 3½"; first I have found not
marked "Rust Craft." Marked: Gibson.
$3.00 – 5.00.

Snips and Snails and Puppy Dog Tails

Boys

With Dog, 6" x 4", flocked. Marked: Norcross. $4.00 – 6.00.

With Puppies, HD 1961, 6½" x 4½", embossed. Marked: American Greetings. $4.00 – 6.00.

Raking Leaves, 6" x 4", flocked. Marked: Norcross. $4.00 – 6.00.

Swinging, 5½" x 4½", flocked. Marked: Norcross. $4.00 – 6.00.

With Dog and Easter Basket, 6" x 5", flocked. Marked: Norcross. $4.00 – 6.00.

Going Down Slide, HD 1964, 5½" x 4½", flocked. Marked: Norcross. $4.00 – 6.00.

Walking with Ducks, 6½" x 4½",
flocked. Marked: Norcross. $4.00 –
6.00.

Climbing Fence, 6¼" x 4½", flocked.
Marked: Hallmark. $4.00 – 6.00.

With Ice Cream and Puppy, 5½" x 4",
flocked. Marked: Hallmark. $4.00 – 6.00.

Hammering a Nail, 7¼" x 4¾", pop-
up. Marked: Gibson. $4.00 – 6.00.

Walking a Fence, 6½" x 4½", flocked.
Marked: Norcross. $4.00 – 6.00.

Talking to an Easter Chick, 5½" x
4½", flocked. Marked: Norcross.
$4.00 – 6.00.

Fishing

In Boat, HD 1952, 5½" x 4½", printed on front and back. Marked: Hallmark. $4.00 – 6.00.

With Pole, 6" x 4". Marked: Rust Craft. $4.00 – 6.00.

On Pier, 5½" x 4¼", glitter. Marked: Hallmark. $4.00 – 6.00.

On Bow of Boat, 5½" x 4¾", glitter. $4.00 – 6.00.

In Boat, 5½" x 4½". Marked: Norcross. $4.00 – 6.00.

In Boat with Girl, 5¼" x 3½". Marked: Sunshine Line. $3.00 – 5.00.

Sports

Baseball, 5" x 4", tri-fold, printed on both front and back and showing six different views. Marked: Norcross. $4.00 – 8.00.

Football, 6¾" x 4¼", flocked. Marked: Gibson. $4.00 – 6.00.

Basketball, 8" x 4". Marked: Gibson. $3.00 – 5.00.

Basketball, 6¼" x 4½". Marked: Gibson. $3.00 – 5.00.

Baseball, 5¾" x 4". Marked: Rust Craft. $4.00 – 6.00.

Basketball, 6¼" x 4¼". $3.00 – 5.00.

With Rose in Mouth, 6½" x 3", embossed. Marked: Hallmark. $4.00 – 6.00.

On Treasure Trunk, c. 1945, 6" x 4", attached feather. Marked: Hallmark. $4.00 – 6.00.

Treasure Trunk, 4½" x 4½", coin holder has slots inside for five dimes. Marked: Hallmark. $4.00 – 6.00.

With Weapons, 6" x 4". Marked: Hallmark. $4.00 – 6.00.

With Girl and Trunk, 7" x 4½". $4.00 –
6.00.

With Girl and Trunk, 5¼" x 4½". Marked: The
Wishing Well. $4.00 – 6.00.

When I Grow Up

Shaving, 7½" x 4¾", attached shaving
foam made of white beads. Marked: American Greetings. $5.00 – 10.00.

With Model Planes, 5½" x 4¼", flocked.
Marked: Gibson. $4.00 – 8.00.

Astronaut, 5¾" x 5½". Marked: Wishing Well Greetings. $4.00 – 8.00.

Astronaut, 7¾" x 3¾", flicker movie card, couple on the card dances. Marked: Barker. $4.00 – 8.00.

Magician, 6½" x 4", die-cut. $4.00 – 6.00.

Matador, 7" x 4½". $4.00 – 6.00.

Sugar and Spice and Everything Nice

Girls

In Shop, 6" x 5". $4.00 – 6.00.

Watering Flowers, 7" x 4½". $4.00 – 6.00.

Birthday, c. 1954, 5½" x 4½", embossed. Marked: Greetings Inc. $3.00 – 5.00.

With Flowers, c. 1950, 6" x 5", embossed. Marked: Greetings Inc. $4.00 – 6.00.

On Fence, 5" x 4". Marked: Norcross. $3.00 – 5.00.

With Kitten, HD 1957, 6" x 4¾", glitter. Marked: American Greeting. $4.00 – 6.00.

In Front of Mirror, HD 1946, 6" x 4½", attached girl and mirror. Marked: Golden Bell Greeting Cards. $4.00 – 6.00.

Under Arch, 5¾" x 4¾", pop-up. $4.00 – 8.00.

In Doorway, 5¾" x 4¾". Marked: Sunshine Line. $4.00 – 8.00.

Reading, HD 1946, 5½" x 4½". Marked: Norcross. $4.00 – 6.00.

Musical Notes, HD 1944, 5½" x 4½", ribbon attachment. Marked: Norcross. $4.00 – 6.00.

In Flowered Hat, HD 1945, 4½" x 4", ribbon attachment. Marked: Hallmark. $5.00 – 10.00.

Girls with Dolls

Baby Buggy, 3" x 3¼", party invitation. $2.00 – 3.00.

Baby Buggy, 4½" x 4½". $4.00 – 6.00.

Tea Party, 3½" x 3", party invitation. $2.00 – 3.00.

Baby Buggy, HD 1945, 4¾" x 4¾". $4.00 – 6.00.

Under Christmas Tree, 5" x 4". Marked: Rust Craft. $4.00 – 6.00.

Christmas Dolly, c. 1938. 5" x 3". Marked: Hallmark. $4.00 – 6.00.

Baby Buggy, 5½" x 4½", glitter. Marked: Gatto. $4.00 – 8.00.

Swinging, 5½" x 4¼". $4.00 – 6.00.

Dolly with Sign, 5¾" x 5¾", glitter. Marked: Hallmark. $4.00 – 8.00.

Baby Buggy, HD 1948, 5" x 4", flocked. Marked: The Wishing Well. $4.00 – 6.00.

Girl Cradling Doll, 5¼" x 4". Marked: Gibson. $5.00 – 10.00.

In Matcing Bonnets, 7" x 5". $5.00 – 20.00.

Birthday Doll, 5½" x 4¾". Marked: Hallmark. $5.00 – 10.00.

Birthday Doll, 5½" x 4½", paper doll. Marked: Fairfield. $5.00 – 50.00.

Valentine's Day, 5¼" x 5", punch-out paper doll and clothes. Marked: A-Meri-Card. $4.00 – 8.00.

Valentine's Day, HD 1950, 4¼" x 4¼", punch-out paper doll and clothes. Marked: A-Meri-Card. $4.00 – 8.00.

Girl with Paper Doll, 6" x 4", flocked. Marked: The Wishing Well. $4.00 – 8.00.

Little Helpers

Baking, 5¼" x 4½", tri-fold. Marked: Norcross. $4.00 – 10.00.

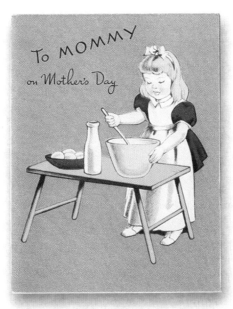

Baking, 4½" x 3½". Marked: Volland. $3.00 – 5.00.

Baking, 5" x 3", novel fold, stand-up. $5.00 – 10.00.

Baking, 6" x 4". Marked: A Sunshine Card. $4.00 – 8.00.

Sewing, HD 1945, 5¾" x 4¾", embossed. Marked: Meryle. $4.00 – 6.00.

Drying Dishes, 5½" x 3". Marked: Gibson. $4.00 – 6.00.

Toys and Games

Toy cards are those that have a toy, trinket, game, puzzle, or other object attached to the front or printed inside. Some have paper dolls to cut or punch out, or something to color with a crayon attached, or perhaps a party balloon or whistle. Children were always excited to find that little something extra with a card. These cards are from a time gone by when kids could play for hours with a punch-out farm, a paper airplane, or a book of dot-to-dot pictures.

Today, collectors prize these cards and especially like to find them as complete boxed sets. A box itself is often found online or in stores; if it's in good shape, buy it. The cards will turn up one at a time till you complete your set.

The popularity of these cards has driven the prices up in recent times. A single toy card may average $3.00 to $10.00, depending of the condition and the quality and how desirable the subject is. A really nice boxed set complete in mint condition can go for over $100, but expect to pay an average of $25 to $50 per set.

Boxed Sets

5¼" x 5¼", box for 12 toy all-occasion cards. Marked: litho'd in Canada. $4.00 – 6.00.

4¾" x 4¾", attached party "wish blower" whistle. Marked: litho'd in Canada. $4.00 – 6.00.

4¾" x 4¾", attached fishing game. Marked: litho'd in Canada. $4.00 – 6.00.

4¾" x 4¾", basket making kit inside. Marked: litho'd in Canada. $4.00 – 6.00.

4¾" x 4¾", dominoes game inside. Marked: litho'd in Canada. $4.00 – 6.00.

4¾" x 4¾", magic pictures inside can be painted with water. Marked: litho'd in Canada. $4.00 – 6.00.

4¾" x 4¾", pop-up elephant ring toss game inside. Marked: litho'd in Canada. $4.00 – 6.00.

4¾" x 4¾", piggy bank with with play money inside. Marked: litho'd in Canada. $4.00 – 6.00.

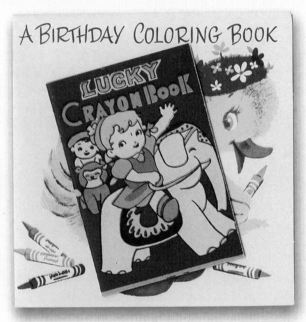

4¾" x 4¾", coloring book attached. Marked: litho'd in Canada. $4.00 – 6.00.

4¾" x 4¾", tattoo transfers inside. Marked: litho'd in Canada. $4.00 – 6.00.

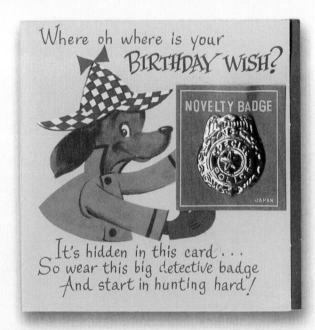

4¾" x 4¾", die-cut windows inside with hidden messages, novelty badge attached. Marked: litho'd in Canada. $4.00 – 6.00.

4¾" x 4¾", toy watch attached. Marked: litho'd in Canada. $4.00 – 6.00.

4¾" x 4¾", inside is a button game board. Marked: litho'd in Canada. $4.00 – 6.00.

6½" x 6½", box for 12 toy cards is an Art Linkletter Favorite Selection. Marked: From the Coronation Collection. $4.00 – 6.00.

6" x 4", bean attached to front of card. Marked: From the Coronation Collection. $4.00 – 8.00.

6" x 4", metal puzzle rings attached to front of card. Marked: From the Coronation Collection. $4.00 – 8.00

6" x 4", party whistle attached. Marked: From the Coronation Collection. $4.00 – 8.00.

6" x 4", instructions inside card for cutting and turning it into a hat. Marked: From the Coronation Collection. $4.00 – 8.00.

6" x 4", toy plastic ship attached. Marked: From the Coronation Collection. $4.00 – 8.00.

6" x 4", riddle card. Marked: From the Coronation Collection. $4.00 – 8.00.

6" x 4", has plastic spoon in mixing bowl. Marked: From the Coronation Collection. $4.00 – 8.00.

6" x 4", Magic Television paint-with-water booklets attached to card. See funny pictures. Marked: From the Coronation Collection. $4.00 – 8.00

6" x 4", picture story card. Marked:
From the Coronation Collection.
$4.00 – 8.00.

6" x 4", instructions inside card to turn it into a jet plane.
Marked: From the Coronation Collection. $4.00 – 8.00.

6" x 4", Covered Wagon Game inside.
Marked: From the Coronation Collection. $4.00 – 8.00 each.

6" x 4", metal whistle attached to card.
Marked: From the Coronation Collection. $4.00 – 8.00 each.

Wheels and Wings and Moving Things

Cars, Go Carts, and Wagons

Valentine, 5¾" x 4½", tri-fold. Marked: G. B. $4.00 – 8.00.

Nephew's Birthday, 4¾" x 4¾". Marked: Hallmark. $4.00 – 8.00.

Birthday, 5¾" x 4½", a double wish card, little dog is removable and has his own greeting. Marked: Wishing Well Greetings. $4.00 – 8.00.

Grandson's Birthday, 6" x 5", flocked. Marked: Norcross. $4.00 – 6.00.

To a Fine Boy, 6" x 4½", tri-fold. Marked: Hallmark. $4.00 – 6.00.

Toy Sailboat, HD 1950, 5½" x 4¼". Marked: Gibson. $4.00 – 6.00.

Model, 6" x 5", flocked. Marked: Norcross. $4.00 – 6.00.

Boy with Cake and Dog, 5½" x 4½", glitter. Marked: Norcross. $4.00 – 6.00.

Children and Dog, 6" x 4¾", glitter, embossed. $4.00 – 6.00.

Boy with Toy, 5½" x 4¼". $4.00 – 6.00.

Bikes and Trikes

Dog in Basket, 6" x 4". Marked: Rust Craft. $4.00 – 6.00.

Boy Delivering Groceries, 5¾" x 4½", embossed. $4.00 – 6.00.

Children and Dog, 6" x 5", glitter. Marked: Friendship Greetings. $4.00 – 8.00.

Hearts in Basket, 6" x 4½". Marked: Hallmark. $4.00 – 6.00.

Child and Heart Flowers, 6" x 4", embossed.
Marked: Hallmark. $4.00 – 6.00.

Boy Doing Tricks, 6" x 4", flocked. Marked: Norcross. $4.00 – 6.00.

Flowers in Basket, 5" x 3¾". Marked: Hallmark.
$3.00 – 5.00.

Child and Mouse, 6½" x 4¼", tri-fold. Marked:
Hallmark. $4.00 – 6.00.

Planes and Things

Valentine, 2½" x 3½", one-sided. Marked: Hall-mark. $2.00 – 4.00.

Valentine, HD 1955, 5¼" x 4". Marked: American Greetings. $4.00 – 6.00.

Birthday, HD 1952, 4¾" x 4½", glitter. Marked: Hall-mark. $4.00 – 8.00.

Birthday, 5" x 4". Marked: A Wishing Well card. $4.00 – 6.00.

Easter, 8½" x 4¼", spaceship originally came with a tiny bag of candy below red bow. Marked: Gibson. $5.00 – 15.00.

Birthday, 5½" x 4½", flocked. Marked: Norcross. $4.00 – 6.00.

Trains

Valentine, HD 1948, 5" x 4". Marked: Forget-Me-Not. $4.00 – 6.00.

For Nephew, 5¾" x 4", glitter. Marked: Gibson. $4.00 – 6.00.

Nephew Birthday, 5" x 5", embossed, tri-fold. Marked: Hallmark. $4.00 – 6.00.

Birthday, 6" x 4", attached neckerchief is made of real fabric. Marked: Norcross. $4.00 – 6.00.

Christmas Toy, 5¼" x 4¼", bright green glitter. Marked: Volland. $4.00 – 6.00.

Duck Conductor, 5½" x 3¼". Marked: Gibson. $3.00 – 5.00.

Zoo, Circus, Carnival, and Other Amusements

The Big Top

Christmas, 5¼" x 4¼". $4.00 – 6.00.

Circus Parade, 4¾" x 4¾", tri-fold, opens to 14¼". $4.00 – 6.00.

Birthday, 5¾" x 4¾". Marked: Grinnel. $4.00 – 8.00.

Valentine, 9" x 5¼", mechanical. Marked: A-MERI-CARD. $5.00 – 12.00.

Lion, 6" x 5", lion's head tilts side-to-side, eyes roll up. $4.00 – 8.00.

Lion in Cage, 5¼" x 4½", tri-fold circus train. Marked: Norcross (a Circus card). $4.00 – 6.00.

Birthday, 9½" x 5¾", easel back. $5.00 – 12.00.

Birthday Camel, c. 1946, 5½" x 4¼", tassel attached. Marked: Charles Christian Culp. $4.00 – 6.00.

Pony Doing Trick, c. 1948, 5¾" x 4½", "5 Years Old" pin-back button attached. Marked: Hallmark. $4.00 – 6.00.

Clowns

Valentine, HD 1945, 5½" x 4½". Marked:
American Greetings. $4.00 – 8.00.

Birthday, c. 1954, 5½" x 4½", embossed.
Marked: Greetings Inc. $4.00 – 8.00.

Birthday Duo, 6" x 3¼", glitter.
Marked: Gibson. $3.00 – 5.00.

With Dog, HD 1945, 5½" x 4½", 3-D pop-out.
$4.00 – 8.00.

Hobo, 5¾" x 4½", dial turns to change
clown's face from smile to frown. Marked:
American Greetings. $4.00 – 6.00.

With Puppets, 5" x 4". Marked: Volland. $3.00 – 5.00.

On Unicycle, 6¼" x 3¼", glitter. Marked: Rust Craft. $3.00 – 5.00.

With Performing Dog, 5¾" x 4¾", glitter. Marked: Forget-Me-Not . $4.00 – 8.00.

With Cake, HD 1965, 6¼" x 3¾", glitter. Marked: Rust Craft. $3.00 – 5.00.

Doing Tricks, HD 1959, 6¼" x 4¾", dial turns to show the illness, embossed. Marked: Sterling. $4.00 – 6.00.

**In Silly Hat, HD 1946, 4½" x 3½".
Marked: Volland.** $2.00 – 4.00.

Animal Acts

Elephant in Washtub, 4½" x 4½", glitter. Marked: Hallmark. $4.00 – 6.00.

With Children, 6¾" x 4¾", glitter. $3.00 – 5.00.

Balancing Bear, HD 1954, 6" x 5", bear and umbrella are attached. Marked: Comics on Parade. $4.00 – 6.00.

Elephant and Mouse, 5¾" x 4". Marked: Hallmark. $4.00 – 6.00.

Elephant with Barrel, c. 1949, 6½" x 4½". Marked: Stanley. $5.00 – 10.00.

Flowered Elephant, 7" x 5", tabs for standing card up. $5.00 – 10.00.

American Greetings, Inc., c. 1949, 5¾" x 4¾".
Marked: Forget-Me-Not. $4.00 – 8.00.

American Greetings, Inc., c. 1949, 5¾" x 4¾".
Marked: Forget-Me-Not. $4.00 – 8.00.

American Greetings, Inc., c. 1949, 5¾" x 4¾".
Marked: Forget-Me-Not. $4.00 – 8.00.

American Greetings, Inc., c. 1949, 5¾" x 4¾".
Marked: Forget-Me-Not. $4.00 – 8.00.

American Greetings, Inc., c. 1949, 5¾" x 4¾". Marked:
Forget-Me-Not. $4.00 – 8.00.

American Greetings, Inc., c. 1949, 5¾" x 4¾".
Marked: Forget-Me-Not. $4.00 – 8.00.

American Greetings, Inc., c. 1949, 5¾" x 4¾". Marked:
Forget-Me-Not. $4.00 – 8.00.

American Greetings, Inc., c. 1949, 5¾" x 4¾".
Marked: Forget-Me-Not. $4.00 – 8.00.

Kiddie Toy Circus Cards (The Biggest Little Show on Earth)

These were created exclusively by Treasure Masters in 1948. The zebra and elephant pictured here are from a series of 12 circus cards. They are designed to stand on their own or be hung on a wall. A removable tab was attached to each; a colorful cardboard 16" x 20" circus tent was free with 12 tabs or 25¢ with 6 tabs. A unique set, but scarce. Cards are 8¼" x 6½" and marked "Treasure Masters." $5.00 – 25.00 each.

Twelve great performers in the Circus collection:

#1 Johnny the Ring Master
#2 Betty Jean the Circus Queen
#3 Leo the Mighty Lion
#4 Jumbo the Elephant
#5 Big Ben the Tiger
#6 Stripey the Zebra

#7 Bowlegs the Bear
#8 Mickey the Monkey
#9 Flapper the Trained Seal
#10 Trixie the Trained Dog
#11 Silver King the Educated Horse
#12 Funny Face the Clown

Stripey the Zebra, 8¼" x 6½".

Jumbo the Elephant, 8¼" x 6¾".

About the Author

Collecting has been a lifelong passion of mine. The earliest collection I can remember was in a Quaker Oats box; the box was filled with bright red and green plastic Missouri tax tokens. I can remember dumping the tokens out, sorting them, and putting them back, over and over. I was maybe four years old at the time. Many different collections have come and gone over the years, but greeting cards have always held a special place in my life.

My greeting card collection started even before my tax token collection. My aunt was the card lover in the family, and she saved for me every card I ever received. I can remember being very young (sometime in the 1940s) and standing next to her at the card counter and looking at all the brightly colored cards while she picked out just the right card for someone. I loved them all, but the cards with dolls, dogs, and horses and the cowboy heroes of the day were some of my favorites. Many of my first cards are included in this book. The little girl in a bonnet on the front cover is from my first birthday. The little girl in red pajamas on the back was from my first Christmas, in 1944.

After I was grown and married, I continued to save cards. Included here are some from the early 1960s that were sent to my son. So I guess you could say I have always loved cards, always saving those that were received and picking up one here and there just because it made me smile. But it wasn't until I discovered eBay that my collection really grew. There are thousands of vintage cards listed every day, and greeting cards have now become one of the fastest growing collectibles.

There is so much more to learn about the cards we all love to collect, the artists who designed them, and the companies that made them. As they are in the section in this book dealing with "Angela" cards, many cards are signed with just a single name. I have tried every lead I have to identify Angela, but without much success. If you have information about Angela or other card artists, I would love to hear from you.

Searching the Internet will turn up several interesting card sites. One good place to start is collectibles.about.com, where you will find information on card collecting and links to some great card websites. You can also email me at oldgreetingcards@bellsouth.net.